THE eSports REVOLUTION - How Visionary Brands Connect with Gen Z

LG Jaeger

D1444520

Dedication

This book is dedicated to the dreamers and the believers and for those who are manifesting their life with a vision in their heart, a song on their lips, and a kindness in their soul.

This book is dedicated to the gamers and esports athletes who are building a brand new multi-billion-dollar industry with their dedication, talent and passion.

This book is dedicated to my father, with love.

Acknowledgment

SPECIAL THANKS TO THE FOLLOWING WONDERFUL CONTRIBUTORS TO THIS PROJECT

Wayne Kimmel - Managing Partner, SeventySix Capital

Jonathan Sumers – Senior Director, Digital Partnerships and Esports Operations at the Cleveland Cavaliers

John Davidson – Founder and CEO of DLC, Chairman of the Esports Trade Association

Anthony Muraco – General Manager, Director of Esports Business Operations for Seattle Surge and Vancouver Titans (Canucks Sports and Entertainment)

Ari Fox - CEO , Casino Esports Conference and Host of the podcast "New Gaming News"

Jorge Tatto – Executive Director of Marketing at CSL Esports, a division of Cineplex

LG Jaeger can be reached at **LG@jaegervo.com**.

About the Author: LG Jaeger

The author behind one of the highly anticipated books is none other than LG Jaeger. LG Jaeger is the Managing Partner and Founder of Esports City Ventures, a consultancy and sponsorship representation agency that connects traditional brand advertisers with Gen Z by introducing esports as an authentic platform leveraging esports athletes, influencers, publishers, and venues. He is also involved in the design and development of esports arenas and esports lounges. LG is a serial entrepreneur who has founded multiple start-ups in the SaaS and sponsorship space. He is proud of a pedigree that includes working for some of the largest technology companies in the world, including Apple, Intel, Samsung and Salesforce. LG is licensed as a certified sports agent, and is available to esports athletes for marketing representation.

Preface

The prevalence of online gaming and esports is thriving, with network connectivity and digital natives playing a vital role in the growth of the industry.

Gaming popularity and competitive esports now entertain millions of live viewers. Today, the video gaming experience has evolved to become more interactive, more social, and more real-time, making it a billion-dollar industry.

This book will enable the reader to understand the aesthetics of the industry, and will explain how visionary brands are making strategic decisions on how to leverage esports to connect with Gen Z.

Contents

Page Left Blank Intentionally

Chapter 1: Introduction

*"But a new generation is on the rise, and the first step to communicating with them is understanding they aren't just another Millennial." -**Pamela La Gioia***

Tiger Woods stood over a three-foot putt on the 18th hole at the infamous Augusta National Country Club. It was the final day of the 2019 MASTERS tournament. It was also 1,715 days since Woods had last won a tournament, (the WSG Firestone National in 2014), and 14 years since his last Masters win in 2005. In that span of time, he had dealt with eight major knee and back surgeries, entire seasons missed, and a scandalous divorce. But none of that mattered at this moment because if Tiger sank this easy putt, he would be the 2019 Masters Champion. Woods did sink the putt and with tears in his eyes he accepted the Masters trophy and with it became golf's first $2 million-dollar prize winner in Master's history. Fred Ridley, the chairman of Augusta National Golf Club and the Masters Tournament called it "an epic Sunday and a historic day for golf".

In that same year, 16-year-old Kyle "Bugha" Giersdorf beat out over 40 million players online and survived six rounds of intense in-person competition for the Fortnite World Cup to become world champion. His prize winnings? A cool $3 million dollars.

So, how does a 16-year old kid win a million bucks more than one of the best golfers of all-time in one tournament? Stay tuned and I'll tell you. That my friends is the power of esports!

There is no secret or surprise to the way the internet and technology have changed our world. We are more connected than ever. You can keep up with your friends and family and find out what they're doing, whether they live 10 minutes or 10 hours away. The devices in our pockets now have replaced maps and dictionaries and modified the way we speak or express ourselves. If a person from the 1930s were to spend a day in 2020, he would quite frankly be blown away by the technical advancements. Or even a person from 1980 for that matter.

The time of our predecessors was one where cell phones did not exist, where if you wanted to play sports, you would gather a group of friends and play under the scorching sun. As the earth has aged, so has technology. The digital revolution did not just come bearing new devices. It changed and transformed people's lives entirely. They went from hanging out with friends whilst being mentally and physically present to meeting up just to take a few selfies and be on their phones. When you're away from your friends you're on your phone, and when you're with your friends you're on your phone. In years past, if you moved away from your loved ones, it was hard to even contact them again.

Those friends more or less disappeared from your life. With all the progressions made, and that social media has made, talking to anyone in any part of the world has become effortless. Video gaming with peers around the globe is not only possible, but is commonplace. Gone are the days when people bought vinyl records whenever an artist they liked released an album. Our new generation relies on Spotify and Apple Music and streaming for all kinds of music. Content is consumed not from television news shows and newspapers, but on Twitter and other social platforms. Gen Z (the group of people born after 1996), are not only consumers, but creators of content on Instagram, Snapchat and Tik Tok.

Most importantly, unlike their predecessors, Gen Z is one where esports are an integral part of their culture. This phenomenon is basically the entire fulcrum of this book.

What are esports?

In the generation today, where technology is everything, sports are now digital. Esports is the abbreviation for electronic sports. There are properly organized events where multiplayer video game competitions between professional players, individually, or as teams, are held. Although organized competitions are not a relatively new idea, they have always existed in the video game culture. Only recently have they reached heights of popularity while generating billions of dollars. In the late 2000s, professional gamers started partaking in these events, and through live streaming, spectatorship attracted millions of people. By the end of 2010, esports became a significant factor in the video game industry. Countless developers actively design and provide funding for their tournaments and other events.

According to Wayne Kimmel, Managing Partner of SeventySix Capital, "The most exciting trend in esports is the blurring of the lines between traditional sports and esports." SeventySix Capital is a leading venture capital firm investing at the epicenter of esports, sports betting and technology. Nerd Street Gamers is a marquee example of this type of investment. Wayne notes that this blurring of the lines is evident as traditional athletes are becoming some of the top streamers in the industry and are now starting to join some of the top esports teams and organizations. As Wayne describes it, "Young people today see streamers and esports athletes the same way previous generations viewed traditional athletes like Michael Jordan, Serena Williams, and LeBron James." Gaming is no longer nerdy, but deemed "cool" by the masses.

The video game genres that are most common within esports include multiplayer online battle arena (MOBA), first-person shooter (FPS), fighting, card games, battle royales, and real-time strategy (RTS). Popular esport franchises include League of Legends, Dota, Counter-Strike, Overwatch, Super Smash Bros., and StarCraft, among many others. What was once just a fringe hobby, now is projected to reach an audience of over 380 million viewers and generate an industry-wide $1.4 billion by the end of 2021. You might wonder where all this money goes. Just like traditional sports – football, soccer, or cricket, esports has fans as well as other stakeholders. These stakeholders include the players, teams, and even the game developers. Moreover, it also has its own share of professionals, commentators, and celebrities. Dedicated channels of content have been created on platforms such as YouTube and Twitch.

The prize money won in esports is surely comparable to other traditional sports. The prize pool for The National Basketball Association is $13 million. For the Golf Masters, it is $11 million, while for FIFA Confederations Cup it stands at $20 million. Esports, on the other hand, tops all of them. It has a total prize pool of $24.7 million. Its rising popularity has come to the point that in a groundbreaking move, the International Olympic Committee has commissioned esports as an official medal sport and will debut at the 2022 Asian Games Olympics, based in Hangzhou, China. In the Olympic Museum in France, an esports forum is planned to be hosted by the IOC and the Global Association of International Sports. This is just the gist of how esports has hijacked the markets.

Esports have changed how we compete with one another; it is the information revolution's reinvention of competition. Online, anywhere, anytime.

Esports is the cultural phenomena based on the competition, community, and entertainment that we see around the world of video games. Anthony Muraco, who has been the Director of Operations for esports for the Cleveland Cavaliers and the Dallas Mavericks, and most recently was the General Manager and Director of Esports Business Operations for the Seattle Surge and Vancouver Titans shared this thought, "The most noticeable trend that is relevant to the growth of esports is the impact that gaming is now having as a lifestyle brand and pop culture way of life." He rightly notes that we have seen the transition over the past few years of every major influencer, athlete, and artist expressing their interest in gaming and live streaming. Esports has partnerships with Juju Smith-Schuster, Post Malone, Logic, Snoop Dogg, and Travis Scott, among others. The roles have reversed, and gaming is now considered the "cool" cultural platform. Gamers are now given massive salaries, and the arenas are almost always sold out.

It is a multi-billion-dollar industry that everyone is only now becoming aware of. In 2020, when the coronavirus pandemic crisis crippled the world and shut down all live, professional sporting events, esports gaming thrived and filled the void of content. NASCAR eRacing was broadcast in prime time on Fox. Streaming numbers on Twitch and YouTube grew exponentially. Competitive video games are being played by professionals, and hundreds and millions of enthusiastic fans worldwide can connect and communicate while watching their favorite gamers, influencers, or teams play.

Even games that professional or celebrity players play from the comfort of their own homes are streamed live by millions of people. The experience is somewhat like watching LeBron James play basketball at his home while interacting with him. I think my friend Anthony Muraco said it best when he shared that kids used to grow up wanting to be a fireman, policeman or professional athlete. Now, many of them are growing up wanting to be gaming content creators or professional esports players.

The Players

The highest sources of income for esports players are the tournaments they partake in. There are competitions held for a cash prize - and the numbers are huge. A German professional Dota 2 player, Kura Salehi Takhasomi, has raked in over $4 million just by winning tournaments. He won over $2 million from a single tournament back in 2017. Moreover, in 2017 alone, $112 million of prize money was actually awarded throughout the year to winning Fortnite players. Epic Games projected $150 million in prize money for the 2020-21 seasons.

Interestingly, winning tournaments, while glamorous, is not a consistent revenue source because you cannot always guarantee to win. Therefore, quite a lot of players actually stream their games on streaming platforms Twitch or YouTube, where viewers can purchase a subscription for a price as cheap as $4.99 per month. The person whose video is being streamed gets half of that money. So, if someone has 4000 subscribers, they can easily make $120,000 per year. This naturally means that top streamers make a much higher amount of money - some reported making $100,000 per month.

While this is a huge sum of money, there's still more to the story. Game streamers also have the option to upload their recorded streams on YouTube. This way, when they get a certain number of subscribers and hit a high number of views, they generate more revenue. Moreover, many streamers actually have fans so loyal that they just donate money to them for no particular reason other than being loyal followers bringing up to $5000 per day. Streamers can also acquire partnerships with different brands, both endemic (specifically video game related) and non-endemic (general consumption brands), promising to promote their products on their channels. All they have to do is share links to that product, and they get paid for that. Like professional football or basketball players, top-ranking esports players are signed to teams as well, which results in another source of income. The starting salary for North America League of Legends Championship Series player is actually over $320,000 - this is comparable to Major League Soccer (MLS) athletes. Teams have started to offer things like health insurance and full benefits.

The Teams

If you want to understand how esports teams make money, all you have to do is contrast them with traditional sports teams. You will see the differences easily. Traditional sports teams generally have huge stadiums and regional fanbases. Esports are streamed online, which means the fanbases are not as localized. Consequently, where traditional sports teams generate revenue by selling tickets to fans coming to their home stadiums, esports lack that advantage. Esports teams thus cannot get income from there, (although teams and investors are building stadiums for in-person watch events).

The luxury that traditional sports teams have of owning broadcasting rights to their games is something esports teams are generally deprived of. An example would be how in 2011, the Los Angeles Lakers signed a 20-year contract with Time Warner Cable for local television rights. The entire deal generated $4 billion, which meant an average of $200 million per year. Esports teams have far less leverage in this aspect. Riot Games (the developer of League of Legends) declined a petition submitted by several esports teams for sharing of revenues and having broadcasting rights.

Esports teams generate most of their money through sponsorship deals, which is estimated to be anywhere from 40% to upwards of 95% of the team revenue. According to research, in 2019 an estimated $897 million was generated through sponsorship, advertising and media rights deals in the esports industry. Although the profits are hefty, there is one problem with such one-sided revenue. Esports is an industry where change is rapid and unpredictable. A team can be popular one day and lose its fame the next, which ultimately causes them to devalue in front of sponsoring companies.

The trend of esports viewership has risen vastly and attracted millions of dollars in capital. The revenue is even brought in through selling merchandise such as branded shirts, hoodies, mouse pads, and other gaming equipment. Additionally, there are now team-customized digital skins, which also project a potential source of revenue. There have been countless investments already made and so much potential for future growth in this industry. This has given esports teams valuations that have skyrocketed, and many estimates show it as

$100-$200 million. The number is expected to increase substantially over the next several years.

The Game Developers

As we discussed earlier, a cash prize is paid to the winner of some of the game developers. Although they are not cheap to host at all and are heavy on the pocket - they produce publicity for the games. Gladly, some of the costs can be covered through ticket sales, advertisements, and sponsorships. Furthermore, broadcasting rights are owned by the game developers - especially for huge tournaments, and these rights can be worth a lot of money.

Microtransactions are small in-game purchases that have been rising lately. These are features like purchasing of skins on a game like Fortnite. Since these games are free to play for everyone, all the revenue generated is through these in-game purchases. This model is known in app or game development as the "Fremium" model where the app or game is free to download, and revenue is made with in game upgrades and purchases. In fact, in February 2018, Fortnite made $126 million, mostly through in-app visual effect items.

It is important to note that game developers have huge development and research costs, just like pharmaceutical companies. And just like only a few drugs pass approval and finally are put out in the market, only a few games end up gaining popularity. Thus, game developers need to create multiple games together in the hopes that one of them can actually reach heights of popularity and generate massive profits for them.

The esports industry is expected to snowball in the coming years. In 2017, worldwide revenues generated in the esports market amounted to $655 million U.S. dollars. At the pace of 22.3 percent annual growth rate, the market is expected to generate close to $1.8 billion U.S. dollars in revenue by 2022.[1]

This book is not a "Gamers Guide" for people who want to know the ins and outs of video gaming. It is going to be an in-depth analysis of the business aspect

---

[1] *eSports market revenue worldwide from 2012 to 2022* Retrieved from
https://www.statista.com/statistics/490522/global-esports-market-revenue/

of esports, and the study of the significant differences of the current generation (dubbed Gen Z for those born after 1996), and how visionary brands and companies can connect to this audience in authentic ways by embracing the gaming explosion and esports in particular. The markets for everything have been changing, as generations keep evolving. Generation gaps are real and exist between Gen Z and the Millennials. Let's explore some general differences between them.

Gen Z vs. the Millennials

People who belong to Gen Z are those born after 1996. Unlike the Millennials who traveled through a time when cell phones did not exist and adapted to smartphones, Gen Z are digital natives. From the day they were born, they grew up with the internet, smartphones, and other digital devices as part of their daily lives - they have constantly only been adapting to the latest technologies as they come. There have been huge disruptions in different forms of media and entertainment from the older generations to Gen Z. Their mobile usage has kicked up a notch, in addition to applications like Instagram, Snapchat, and Tik Tok, playing sports has now been made digital too. Through the rise of new platforms and applications, we are looking at a significant change in the way media is consumed and how companies make money through it. While they may all look young, people from Generation X (aka Millennials) and Z are considerably different in the ways they shop, view their money, and how they associate with brands.[2]

Millennials are idealistic; Gen Z is pragmatic

Millennials have always been a generation where optimism was on the rise, and today the lives of parents and adults are a reflection of that. Gen Z, on the other hand, grew up in a world marked by major world events that heightened the natural level of fear and uncertainty. Starting with the tragedy of 9/11 in 2001, there has been a never-ending series of disasters that have thrown off the

---

[2]*Millennials vs. Gen Z: How Are They Different?* Retrieved from
https://www.salesforce.com/blog/2017/10/how-Millennials-and-gen-z-are-different.html

natural balance in the world. Massive school shootings such as Columbine and Sandy Hook Elementary Schools have led to a school culture where "live shooter drills" have become as commonplace as "nuclear bomb drills" were during the cold war. The news and social media bombard the senses with graphic scenes like the shootings in Las Vegas in 2017, where a gunman with automatic weapons opened fire from a sniper's nest on the 32nd floor of a high-rise hotel, killing 59 and wounding more than 850 spectators at a country music concert. In 2007, 32 people died and 17 were wounded at Virginia Tech University from a deranged gunman. Airplanes disappear from the skies and murder rates continue to sky rocket.

The worst recession in recent history rocked the world economy in 2008. And in 2020, the coronavirus pandemic, (COVID 19) shut down civilization as we know it for almost the entire year and beyond, changing life now and into the foreseeable future. Gen Z has only known a world of amazing technology, but also a world of metal detectors, live shooter drills and mandatory mask requirements. Naturally, Gen Z is a more cautious and anxious class of individuals, steering as far from risky behaviors as possible.

They make smart career choices and have stats proving lower underage drinking and a higher seatbelt wearing in this group. The Millennials were raised amid an economic boom, Gen Z, on the other hand, grew up during the recession that started in 2008 and lasted many years thereafter. The economic pressure that may have occurred when they were younger has shaped this generation. They are more focused on long-term value, creating their own opportunities, and smart investments. Since economics is more uncertain, and career paths are less defined, this generation has become the generation of the "Gig Economy". The gig economy is fueled by multiple jobs such as Uber or Door Dash drivers, freelance opportunities and creating their own influencer brands on social media.

Millennials want a good experience; Gen Z wants to save money

The teenagers today are more interested in being financially smart than Millennials were at that age. For Millennials, the entire experience of buying a product is what matters the most, which is where their priorities lie. Gen Z, on the other hand, is smart when it comes to making purchases - they cautiously buy products that maximize the value of every dollar they spend on something. When it comes to money - both these generations have a different attitude. Sure, they both care deeply about their finances and invest in things they know can improve their careers; for example, higher education.

However, Gen Z bases its purchases more on the practicality of the products rather than how it would make them feel. This habit of being spending conservatively in the Gen Z era, emerges from growing up at a time when the world was in an economic turmoil. Therefore, conspicuous expenditure is not at all attractive to them. Minimalism is a respected cultural philosophy. They always think about running out of money, thus ensure they save money wherever they get a chance. This is one of the reasons offering deals like 'free shipping' is a smart way to market to them. It's a fact that most people who sign up for Amazon Prime do it for that specific reason alone.

Millennials are pleasantly surprised by innovation; Gen Z expects and even demands innovation from companies

Most Millennials believe companies introduce innovations in products based on what the customers need, what they value, and when there is a need for change. Only 71% of Gen Z happens to agree with this. This is because growing up in an age where new iPhones come out every year; they have become expectant of rapid innovation. Millennials still remember Blockbuster VHS rentals, whereas the era Gen Z lives in a world that allows them to have Netflix on their phones. Gen Z doesn't ever have to leave the cave and forage for content, as content comes to them.

Millennials love to aspire for well-polished perfection, Gen Z cares a bit too much about authenticity

While Millennials have always preferred brands that advertise transparency and walk the talk, authenticity is something Gen Z literally worships. They are fully obsessed with discovering brands that feel "authentic." An example of this is the clothing company American Eagle. They shared that their 'no-Photoshop' policy, has resonated deeply with younger teens. (Whereas for Millennials the half-naked, highly photoshopped images in Abercrombie or Victoria Secret advertisements were what resonated the most.) Gen Z is bent on seeing content that is not fake or does not look staged. They do not idealize a world where everything is perfect - thus, they want to see reality for what it is; flawed, attainable, and raw.

Their Attitudes towards Technology differ

One of the most obvious differences I have subtly inferred to earlier are the technological differences between the eras each generation was brought up in. Millennials grew up using giant desktop computers, cell phones with antennas or flip phones with no screens, dial-up internet, and DVD players. At that time, we thought technology had peaked. What could ever top a phone that folds in half? Kids in Gen Z, on the other hand, were essentially born with iPads in their hands. Most teens have access to smartphones, ubiquitous Wi-Fi, and services like Netflix, which has put previous technology to shame. While Millennials saw the birth of innovation, Gen Z was born into it.

Additionally, Gen Z has also been called the "socially-conscious-generation." They have been known to deal with more mental health, cyberbullying, and body shaming issues than any other generation. Furthermore, regardless of all their digital connectivity, they are also known to be the loneliest generation.

Concluding what we have discussed so far, my aim is that the readers get to learn a lot from this book. We started with a deep dive into the historical aspect of esports. Moving ahead, we explored in depth the audience that esports captures. Moreover, unlike this brief overview of the differences between Gen Z and the Millennials, we will move on and explore every generation from baby boomers to Gen Z. As we discuss each generation, included will be the best marketing techniques for each group and how to approach them best. Towards the end, we will look at an overview of the different types of advertisements and how they have evolved in the digital age. An important aspect of that is who social media influencers are and how they can be used to connect with Gen Z in a better way. Lastly, I will touch base with what sponsorship is, how it differs from advertisement, and how it can be used to a brand's advantage.

This book will take a serious, in-depth look at the **BUSINESS SIDE** of esports and the rapid acceleration of dollars being invested to this new industry, and sponsorship and advertising dollars that both endemic (gaming companies) and non-endemic (traditional brands) are spending to reach the very elusive GENERATION Z audience.

All of these concepts may sound like a lot to tackle, but trust me, as you keep turning the pages it'll only get easier to understand and more compelling!

Chapter 2: The History of Gaming

"Gaming IS culture today, and esports is the competitive aspect of it." So says John Davidson, Founder and CEO of DLC, an esports consulting firm in Dallas. John is also the Chairman of the Esports Trade Association. The blending of music, sports and esports has created the Gen Z culture of today. As John points out, "The most viewed concerts are now those embedded into video games, such as Travis Scott and Fortnite". But how did video gaming and esports become such the cultural phenomenon that it is today?

Video games, like everything else, have developed and revolutionized over the decades. What was just a purely technical definition before, is now an entirely new class of interactive entertainment. In fact, they make up a $100 billion global industry, and over two-thirds of household members of American homes play video games regularly. It is not a surprise. For decades video games have been around, traversing the scale of platforms; from home and handheld consoles to full blown arcade systems. More often than not, they are also at the vanguard of computer technology.

Technically, for a product to be a video game, a video signal must be broadcasted to a video display of some sort. Originally these were CRT's (cathode ray tubes) that created a rasterized image on a screen. In computer graphics a rasterized image is a dot matrix data structure that represents generally a grid of pixels. This representation impeded early computer games executed on a vector-scan monitor, games played on a modern high-definition display, and most handheld game systems. From a technical viewpoint, these were more accurately called "electronic games" or "computer games." Today the displays are more advanced and are usually either LED (light-emitting diode) or LCD (liquid-crystal display).

Today, however, the term "video game" has dropped its purely technical definition and incorporates a broader range of technology. While still rather ill-defined, the term "video game" now generally includes any game played on devices built with electronic logic circuits that consolidates an element of interactivity and outputs the results of the player's actions to a display, including mobile devices. Going by this broader definition, the first video games appeared in the early 1950s and were mainly tied to research projects at universities and large corporations. In this chapter, we will dive a little into the history of video games and gaming consoles.

Origins of Electronic Computer Games

The first electronic digital computers, Colossus and ENIAC, were built during World War II to aid the Allied war effort against the Axis powers. Shortly after the war, the promulgation of the first stored-program architectures started at the University of Manchester (Manchester Mark 1), Cambridge University (EDSAC), the University of Pennsylvania (EDVAC), and Princeton University (IAS machine).

This allowed computers to be easily reprogrammed to undertake a variety of tasks, which facilitated commercializing computers in the early 1950s by companies like Remington Rand, Ferranti, and IBM. This, in turn, elevated the adoption of computers by universities, government organizations, and large corporations as the decade progressed. It was in this environment that the first video games were born.

The computer games of the 1950s can generally be divided into three categories: training and instructional programs, research programs in fields such as artificial intelligence, and demonstration programs intended to impress or entertain the public. Since these games were extensively developed on uncommon hardware when porting between systems was tricky and often demolished or discarded after serving their limited purposes, they did not generally affect further developments in the industry. For the same reason, it is impossible to be certain who developed the first computer game or who originally modeled many of the games.

The First Video Game

In October 1958, physicist William Higinbotham created what was thought to be the first video game. It was a straightforward tennis game, similar to the classic 1970s video game Pong, and it was quite a hit at a Brookhaven National Laboratory open house.

Higinbotham took only a few hours to formulate the idea of a tennis game, and just a few days to combine the basic pieces. Since he had previously operated displays for many electronic devices and radar systems, designing a simplistic game display was not a problem for him. In no time, he had created some drawings and formed blueprints. It took two weeks to build the device, and after a little debugging, the first video game ever was prepared for its premiere. The game was called Tennis for Two.

Players were able to adjust the angle of the ball and press the button to hit the other player's ball. As long as they press the button when the ball is in their court, the players can't miss the ball, but if they hit the wrong time or hit it to the left, the ball won't make it over the net. The ground balls were riding like a real tennis ball. When the ball came out of the court, players hit the reset button to start the next round.

Tennis for Two did not have a high-quality video display like the ones available today. The cathode ray tube signal just showed the side of the tennis court represented by two rows, one representing the ground and the other representing the net. The ball was just a dot that ran back and forth. The players also had to keep score. The game's rotation was simple, mainly using resistors, capacitors, and transmitters, using the transistors for the fast switches needed when the ball was played. Although Tennis for Two was invented first, a game called Spacewar was invented soon after which got far more attention than the former.

Invention of Spacewar

*"If I hadn't done it, someone would've done something equally exciting, if not better, in the next six months. I just happened to get there first."- **Steve Russell, aka "Slug" on inventing Spacewar***

Steve Russell was a young computer programmer from MIT and the creator of Spacewar. Back in 1962, headed up the team that created the first popular computer game. The team took approximately 200 man-hours to draft the first version of Spacewar.

Russell wrote Spacewar on PDP-1, the first DEC (Digital Equipment Corporation) computer-based system that used a cathode-ray tube type display and keyboard input. DEC provided the computer to MIT, hoping that MIT's think tank would be able to do something amazing with its product. The Spacewar computer game was the last thing the DEC executives had hoped for, but they later offered the game as a diagnostic program for their customers.

How did it work?

The PDP-1 operating system was the first to allow multiple users to share a computer at one time. This was ideal for playing Spacewar, which was a two-player game that combines combat spaces and shooting photon torpedoes. Each player used the atmosphere and gained points by firing their arrows while avoiding direct sunlight.

Dawn of the Home Console

In August 1966, Ralph Baer considered the idea of a dedicated video game console, and spent the next three years creating the prototype. The 'Brown Box' was the seventh of these prototypes to be created. Many different manufacturers were shown this system before Magnavox approved its production in January 1971. It is the first commercial video home console ever built. Baer is considered the father of video games due to his many contributions to video games that helped spark the video game revolution. In 2006, Baer was awarded the National Medal of Technology for his groundbreaking and pioneering creations and help in commercializing the video game industry.

The Brown Box, was released commercially as the Odyssey console in September 1972 by Magnavox in the United States and other countries the following year. Since its release, Magnavox sold approximately 100,000 pieces by the end of the year. And 350,000 when the console was end of life'd in 1975.

The Odyssey contained three boxes; white, black, and brown, connecting to a television set with two cable controllers. It was capable of displaying three square dots on the screen in monochrome black and white, with different behavior on the dots depending on the game being played. Players put a plastic overlap on the screen to create the visual, and one or two players in each game control their dots with three sticks and one button on the controller according to the rules given to the game. The Odyssey console came bundled with dice, paper money, and other board-related items to accompany the games, and the peripheral controller - the first video light gun - was sold separately. The console featured the Odyssey series of dedicated consoles, culminating with the 1978 Magnavox Odyssey. One of the 28 games designed for the program, the ping pong game, was the inspiration for Atari's successful Pong Arcade game.

Atari Releases Pong

After getting inspired by Magnavox Odyssey's ping-pong electric game, Atari released their version, Pong, in 1972. Pong was a table tennis game featuring two-dimensional drawings. It was one of the most widely played video games and invented by Allan Alcorn. The player controlled the paddle of the game and played against a computer-controlled opponent or another player. Players used short bars to hit the ball back and forth. The game was played exactly like real life Ping Pong. Players earned more points than his competitors, scored when a person cannot return the ball to another.

Pong delivered four times more revenue than other video game competitors. This provided Atari with a consistent revenue as the company sold the equipment at three times the cost of production. Full blown arcade cabinets have always been a collector's item, and the table top version has become rare. Atari eventually sold more than 35,000 units. This spawned many imitations from competitors.

With Pong's success as an arcade game, Atari decided to create new products. In 1974, Atari engineer Harold Lee proposed a Pong home model that would connect to a television: Home Pong. It was an immediate success following its 1975 limited edition, sold by Sears just in time for the holidays, an estimated sale of 150,000 units was sold. That game became their most successful product at the time, which led to Atari receiving the Sears Quality Excellence Award.

This resulted in a Lawsuit...

In 1972 Ralph Baer, founder of the Magnavox Odyssey sued Atari. Baer said that Atari's founder, Nolan Bushnell, had copied Magnavox's electronic plan for Ping-Pong after Bushnell had played the game in the Magnavox retail market just months before Pong was released. Due to copyright infringements, Magnavox has generated three times as much profit by filing lawsuits against many other sports companies that allegedly violated the "Baer law" than it did in actually selling the Odyssey. Magnavox abandoned the Odyssey in 1975 - having sold 350,000 units worldwide at a $ 100 retail price, or $ 50 when purchased together with Magnavox TV. All told, Magnavox has won over $100 million in lawsuit cases alone.

Atari 2600

Atari released the Atari 2600 in September 1977, which is also recognized as the initial Video Computer System. It is a home video game console and is credited with spreading the use of microprocessor-based hardware and games stored on ROM cartridges (a format first used with the Fairchild Channel F in 1976) instead of dedicated hardware with games physically built into the unit. The Atari 2600 came with two joystick controllers, an integrated pair of paddle controllers and game cartridges. The first games sold were initially Combat and later Pac-Man.

The Atari VCS started with nine simple, low-resolution games in two KiB cartridges. In 1980, they launched Titus Attackers. The program became so popular that it led to the production of *Activision* and other third-party developers and competition from local companies such as Mattel and Coleco. Towards the end of its original lifecycle in 1984, games that were created for 2600 started to use more than four times the ROM of the original launch. The game touted significantly better visuals and gameplay. Examples of early games for this platform were Pitfall, and its sequel Pitfall II: Lost Caverns. There were two games Atari had made heavy investments in; Pac-Man and ET, the Extra-Terrestrial.

Pac-Man

A game only an alien would not know of. In the United States, this came out on May 21, 1980, and released in Japan by October of the same year. We are all familiar with its gameplay - a yellow, pie-shaped Pac-Man character, which encompasses a maze in attempts to eat dots, all the while dodging four hunting ghosts. In no time, it became an iconic symbol of the 1980s.

For the Atari 2600, Pac-Man was released in 1982. Atari developed and published the game under authorized license by Namco. Atari already expected the sales to be high, thus producing one million copies for its launch. That was not all - they also held a "National Pac-Man Day" to boost the promotion of its release.

Even after all these years, it stands as Atari 2600's best-selling game of all time. It has been estimated to sell around 7 million copies worldwide. Even though it did spectacularly on a commercial scale, many critics trashed it for low-quality sound and visuals. Additionally, they also said it bore minimal similarities to the original game.

The 1983 Video Game Crash

The video game crash, which also went by the name "Atari Shock" in Japan, was a recession that took place industry-wide. In just two years, the revenues for makers of video games dropped by almost 97%. Due to the crash, the fast-growing industry hit a wall and saw a huge slash in their incomes. In today's economic terminology we would call this the bubble. There were too many companies that had high hopes about gaming and so tried to find their way in the industry too quickly. An example of this "gold rush' mentality was when companies that were entirely outside of the scope of gaming made efforts to partake and consequently caused huge issues for the industry. The question remains, why *did* it crash?

1. **Quantity over Quality**– Video game corporations couldn't help but formulate as many game cartridges as possible. They also held a belief that entire consoles would be bought by customers just to play a few games. At one point, 12

million cartridges of Pac-Man were created by Atari when it was known that only 10 million people owned an Atari 2600. Seven million copies were ultimately sold by the game but had bad reviews. This is the reason Atari was left with five million spare copies in stock.

2.   **Unchecked Competition**– At this point, programmers were capable of reverse engineering and creating unlicensed games. This sparked some nasty conflict, with gaming companies stealing programmers from one another with promises for credit and an unlimited stream of game cartridges inundating the market. Different names were given to the same game, and its copies were published regularly. If you look at it through a modern example, it would be like Nintendo created an Xbox game, and releasing it without permission from Microsoft.

3.   **Economic Inflation**– Inflation and the introduction of new monetary coins in the US market also added to the crash. Arcades struggled with the decline of the American quarter value because customers relied on coins to play arcade games. Arcades even requested to replace the gargantuan Eisenhower dollar with the Susan B. Anthony dollar, which was near the size of the quarter. The new coin, introduced in 1979, was considered a failure because customers complained it looked too much like a quarter.

4.   **Competing Industrie**s– At the time, personal computers and video game consoles were nearly the same prices. PCs could often process video games better, and they had other programming abilities that made them more attractive than video game consoles.

The Aftermath

The video game crash of 1983 eliminated a lot of competition in the industry. It was not just the small-scale companies that went under, full recovery was never made even by the top companies in the gaming industry. However, through all the chaos and downfalls, Nintendo rose from the ashes and forever changed the gaming industry.

Nintendo Entertainment System

Nintendo changed the gaming industry forever by implementing a lock-out chip in their consoles. This lock-out chip was meant to eliminate any unlicensed corporations from making games for their console. This disruptive lock out technology led to their success, the results of which can even be felt today.

The Nintendo Entertainment System (NES) was created in Japan, and sold worldwide starting in 1985 as the first-ever video game console. It was also known as the Famicom or the Family Computer. It gained popularity in no time. It had different controllers as compared to those joysticks the previous gaming consoles had.

It had a D-pad button that could go up, down, left, or right. It also had A, B, Select, and Start buttons. The NES could use up to two controllers for multiplayer games. There were also other types of controllers that could be utilized with the NES. NES had an exclusive on a few world-famous games like The Legend of Zelda, Metroid, Super Mario Bros, Donkey King, Castlevania, Mario Bros, and so on. Many sequels were also created for these games. The NES continued to have record sales right up until production was stopped in 1995.

Technical details

The CPU (Central Processing Unit) in the NES is called MOS 6502 and is an 8-bit CPU. The chip containing the CPU also contains other electronics that generate sound for games and help with other things. There are two different versions of the chip called 2A03 and 2A07 that are used in different regions of the world (2A03 works with NTSC TVs, 2A07 with PAL TVs). It was made by a company called Ricoh. The NES uses a chip called the PPU (Picture Processing Unit) to draw graphics on the TV. It has two different versions called 2C02 (for NTSC TVs) and 2C07 (for PAL TVs). It was also made by Ricoh.

The First Console War

Rewind to 1989 - a 16-bit Genesis console was released by Sega in North America. This was done with the intention of it being a replacement to the Sega

Master System. It found it could not compete against the NES and thus was a failure. Sega ensured to come back bigger and better. It held superiority over the NES through technological advancements and shrewd marketing. Additionally, in 1991 the infamous game Sonic the Hedgehog was also released on the Sega platform, resulting in picking up significant market share.

The real console war was launched in 1991 when Nintendo released its 16-bit Super NES console in North America.

In the mid-to-early 1990s, a wealth of famous games was released on both the consoles. These included new franchises such as Street Fighter II and Mortal Kombat, a fighting game that portrayed blood and carnage on the game's Genesis version.

As a response to this violent game (and also the congressional discussions about violent video games), the Videogame Rating Council was created by Sega in 1993. The intent of this was to provide detailed labeling for any and every game that was sold on a Sega home console. By the mid-1990s, video games took a jump to the Big Screen once Super Mario Bros was released as a live-action movie in 1993. This became a trend as Street Fighter and Mortal Kombat followed as their own movie titles in subsequent years. Ever since then, movies based on video games became a thing. With a much more extensive library of games, cheaper price point, and successful marketing, the Genesis had leapfrogged the competition in North America by this time. But Sega was unable to find a comparable breakthrough in Japan.

The Rise of 3D Gaming

In the mid-90s, the fifth generation of video games were released, this time in the three-dimensional gaming era. The first 32-bit console that played games on CDs instead of cartridges was released in 1995 by Sega on its Saturn System. They wanted to beat Sony's sales for their new console named Playstation, which was scheduled to release later that year. At its release date it sold for $100 less than the Saturn leading to its initial popularity. The next year, Nintendo released its cartridge-based 64-bit system, the Nintendo 64. The wars were on!!

Although Nintendo and Sega both released their due shares of on-brand, highly-rated 3D titles, like Virtua Fighter on Saturn and Super Mario 64 on the Nintendo 64, they could not compete with the strong third-party support Sony had. This strategic positioning gave the PlayStation an edge over them, consequently securing numerous exclusive titles. In other words, Sony overtook the video game market from both companies and has continued to do so even today. In fact, the PlayStation 2, released in 2000 and able to play original PlayStation games, became the best-selling game console of all time.

It was the first console that used DVDs, went up against the Sega Dreamcast (released in 1999), the Nintendo Gamecube (2001), and Microsoft's Xbox (2001). The Dreamcast—considered by many to be technically ahead of its time and one of the most prominent consoles ever made for numerous reasons, including its aptitude for online gaming—was a business flop that ended Sega's console efforts. Sega pulled the plug on the system in 2001, becoming exclusively a third-party software company henceforth.

First eSport tournament

On Stanford's campus, back in October 1972, a few enterprising students kicked off the first eSport tournament. It was nothing fancy, the name of the competition was the 'Intergalactic Spacewar Olympics.' The winner's prize was a subscription to Rolling Stone, the magazine. Amid the very contentious game, players were given a specific number of missiles and fuel. This meant that it was not just a game of strategy, but also of reflexes. The learning curve needed practicing, consistency, and diverse skills making it certainly the founder of the esports games. Stewart Brand, 33 years old, a biology student, was the first person to win this Intergalactic Spacewar Olympics. Consequently, he holds the notable distinction of also being the first player to win a video game tournament.

Esports Today

We have talked about the history of video games, from the first one ever created, to the first esports competition that was ever held. Fast forward to today and we explore the state of esports today. In recent years, esports and gaming have exploded into the mainstream. What was once a vibrant niche has now transformed into a central form of entertainment globally. Even though esports once stood for just a certain subset of sports culture, it has now grown to become a full industry on its own. This shift in esports has been powered by championing from well-known celebrities like Michael Jordan, Drake, and Travis Scott. Thanks to celebrity influencers, these events have gotten extra coverage from outlets that are traditional and popular, like ESPN, and, at least in part is responsible for the breakneck rise of Fortnite.

Esports Market Growth Trends

Global investors, brands, media outlets, and consumers are all paying attention to the competitive gaming proliferation in the modern culture. Between 2019 and 2023, the total esports viewership has been expected to rise at a 9% compound annual growth rate, increasing from 454 million in 2019 to 646 million in 2023. Compared to 2017, it puts the audience on pace to almost double over six years as back then, it stood at 335 million.

The pop-culturization of esports has helped fuel the bursts in esports investment and income. Due to the social component of live streaming and gaming, esports has exploded into the stratosphere in terms of popularity. Fans are given a direct connection to the players and teams through gaming-specific streaming platforms that have been created such as Twitch and Youtube Gaming. Additionally, more mainstream social media platforms have helped those connections to thrive.

FaZe Clan and other similar esports organizations have also started to move aggressively into different areas like merchandise and co-branding, offering their brands more fame than if they only stuck to esports alone.

Esports Industry Investment Outlook

Consequently, the industry has seen a huge uptick in investment from venture capitalists and private equity firms and most recently SPACS. A SPAC is a special purpose acquisition company that is basically a blank check shell corporation designed to take a company public without going through the traditional IPO process. SPACS have become popular mainly because they allow retail investors to invest in private equity type transactions, particularly leveraged buyouts.

The number of investments in esports doubled in 2018, per analyst company Deloitte. That's indicative in the total number of pure dollars funded as well. Deloitte also points out that investments are up to $4.5 billion in 2018 from just $490 million the year prior, a tremendous YoY growth rate of 837%. According to Data Bridge Market Research the overall market will grow over 400% in the next seven years.

The aggregate gaming market is expected to cross a quarter of a trillion dollars in annual revenue by 2025 and investment dollars will continue to follow on this aggressive trajectory. These investments are distributed to players across the ecosystem — from esports organizations to tournament operators, to digital broadcasters — allowing it to perform and develop. In just the past decade, esports has made huge strides evolving from a largely underground culture into a mainstream industry.

Investors like Ashton Kutcher, Shaquille O'Neil, David Beckham and Mark Cuban are investing in the sector. Events such as the League of Legends World Championships matched the Super Bowl in terms of viewership. Young gamers who are digital natives in the extremely desirable Gen Z demographic of 18 -25 years old watch 34% more esports than traditional sports. The net result is that esports has transformed from its origins in arcade gaming to the complex digital ecosystem it is now. With more than 2.7 billion gamers on earth, we are barely scratching the surface of what's possible for the growth of esports.

Chapter 3: The Esports Audience

In the world we live in, change is imminent. The interests that people have, things that trend, and everything else keeps evolving. Over the past ten years, the way consumers "consume" content has transformed drastically. Firstly, instead of watching professionally-created content, people enjoy watching each other play. Secondly, every day their desire to create, share, and ultimately be a part of the whole experience has also been increasing.

This is a culture that everyone can participate in. Esports has grown at an explosive rate. This can be illustrated best by the success of sharing game video content. If we look back to 2005, only 1%[3] of consumers were recognized as creators or "prosumers." Fast forward to ten years later in 2015, every other person started creating and sharing their experiences while earning a good amount of money doing so. By the year 2020, virtually everyone can be a consumer and creator of content.

Growth of Viewers

In recent years, the esports market has attracted more and more viewers and is continuing to do so. In 2012, esports had a total viewership of 134 million[4] (58 million esports enthusiasts and 76 million occasional viewers). Six years later, in 2018, that number shot up to 395 million (of which 173 million were esports enthusiasts and 222 million casual viewers). If you compare the numbers, you will come to a mind-blowing realization that in just six years, the total viewership grew by 195%. Roundhill Investments research projects that esports viewership is expected to grow to 646 million by 2023 (351 million occasional viewers and 295 million esports enthusiasts). This represents a 10.3% CAGR from 2018 - 2023.

---

[3] *The Global Growth of Esports* Retrieved from
https://cdn2.hubspot.net/hubfs/700740/Reports/Newzoo_Preview_Report_Global_Growth_of_Esp orts_Report_FINAL_2.0.pdf
[4] *Esports Viewership* Retrieved from
https://www.roundhillinvestments.com/research/esports/esports-viewership-vs-sports

In 2018, there was an estimate of 25.7 million esports viewers in the United States. It is forecasted that by 2023, this number will rise to over 46 million. This ultimately implies that an estimated 15.5% of internet users by 2023 will be watching esports at least once per month. For an industry that not too long ago was considered to be a niche segment of the gaming market, that is a remarkable number.

Although there is huge potential for the esports industry in the United States, the market size in the Asia Pacific is nothing to be compared to. Estimates have shown that over half of the world's viewers and enthusiasts of esports are from the Asia Pacific region, while only 12% are in North America.

Twitch Revenue and Usage Statistics

In case you do not already know, Twitch is a platform where video games are live-streamed. Justin Kan founded it back in 2011[5], originally as a spin-off of Justin.tv. Within two years, the website had around 45 million unique visitors. Due to this massive number, it was no surprise that Amazon offered to acquire it, seeing how much potential it bore. By August 2014, Amazon bought it for $1 billion, when it had up to 55 million active monthly users and accounted for 1.8% peak internet traffic back then - just behind Apple, Google, and Netflix.

The traffic continued to grow at an expansive rate from there, with 1.5 million broadcasters and 100 million monthly viewers by 2015. By 2018, these numbers grew to 2.2 million broadcasters and 15 million daily viewers - interestingly, at any given time, at least a million users were using the platform. In 2020's first quarter, the average concurrent viewers at any one point in time were up to 1.4 million. The platform is associated with Amazon Prime and enables streamers to earn money by offering in-stream links through which viewers can buy the games being played.

According to the Twitch Tracker, in February 2020, 3.8 million streamers broadcasted on Twitch. In a report released by Twitch just two years prior, there were 2.2 million broadcasters reported. The number of unique daily viewers was

---

[5] *Twitch Revenue and Usage Statistics* Retrieved from
https://www.businessofapps.com/data/twitch-statistics/#1

clinched at 15 million, with monthly users at 140 million. Twitch was easily outstripping MNSBC and CNN when it came to peak concurrent viewership by 2018; 885,000 and 783,000. By March 2020, there was an average of 3.84 million monthly Twitch broadcasters concurrently broadcasting.

Collegiate and High School esports growth

Five years ago, there were only a handful of colleges with esports programs. By the year 2021, there will be over 175. With the gaming industry exploding, savvy schools are attracting new students with a cultural and career interest in this phenomenon. Full Sail University in Orlando, Florida created the Fortress, an indoor venue dedicated exclusively to esports competitions. The Fortress, at 11,200 square feet is the largest collegiate arena for competitive gaming.

Esports has been in explosive growth mode for years, and colleges are getting in on it. Esports is set to surpass $1.5 billion in revenues by 2023, according to the Esports Ecosystem Report, published by Business Insider Intelligence. The number of venture capital investments in esports doubled in just one year, between 2017 and 2018, according to accounting firm Deloitte, representing more than $4.5 billion in actual investment dollars.

Professional teams and gamers are driving that trend, however just like with traditional sports like football, basketball, soccer and baseball a youth system will continue to evolve to allow participation at all ages and to create an ecosystem of highly skilled and developed players as they graduate from high school to college to the pros.

Jorge Tatto is the Executive Director of Marketing at CSL (Collegiate Star League), formerly a division of the Canadian cinema chain Cineplex. Jorge states that one of the most important trends in esports to watch out for are collegiate and high school esports growth and consolidation. He says, "This space has remained relatively untapped. Over the next several years we will start seeing consolidation in the sector." There will be overall government like there is at the NCAA (collegiate) or NFHS (high school) level.

As the CEO and Founder of Esports City, LLC, a consultative sponsorship agency focused on high school sports sponsorships, I personally work with schools and colleges across the country who are creating esports teams, leagues and venues from the ground up. The transition has to pivot from esports being just "club sports" at these levels to actual sanctioned and fully funded sports, including scholarships and a framework that has a proper esports competition infrastructure.

The convergence of esports and gambling...

Betting on esports is in no way a new concept. The handle has grown alongside the proliferation of the sport itself, with the global esports betting market forecast to reach $17.2 billion by the end of 2020, according to Wholesale Investor. Bookmakers are starting to explore the competitive gaming category, while established esports books are seeing massive surges in activity.

Wayne Kimmel's firm, SeventySix Capital is a leader in not only esports, but also at the forefront of sports gambling. I asked Wayne what his projection was for the merging of sports gambling and esports. According to Wayne, esports and sports betting are a match made in heaven. "Fast paced gameplay, variety, and non-stop games makes esports a potential major hit for both casual and sharp bettors." Data is the key to esports gambling being successful so publishers will need to share data with sportsbooks to be able to offer real time odds. Once that occurs, betting lines will be created, more games will be available to bettors, and the quicker the convergence of the two industries will happen. As multimillion-dollar prize pools and online betting becomes prevalent, new rules and structures will be needed to combat cheating and match-fixing. Organizations such as the Esports Integrity Coalition (ESIC) and similar organizations have been formed to help the industry regulate itself.

An Ever-Changing, Hit-Driven Industry...

The thing about esports is that unlike typical sports, it changes way too fast. Every now and then, new games come out and if catchy enough, spread among game enthusiasts like wildfire. For instance, Fortnite and Pubg did not even exist back in 2016. Neither did the Call of Duty World League in its new form or the Overwatch League. Considering Fortnite only came into the market in 2016, it was surprising that when the total hours watched mark of the Final World Cup held in summer 2019 hit 1.8 million. This led to it being at the top of the Twitch charts. In June of 2020, Valorant was released to great fanfare. Valorant is a free-to-play multiplayer tactical first-person hero shooter game developed and published by Riot Games. It has quickly become one of the most popular titles.

Interestingly, Fortnite barely got a chance to claim their viewership sport for more than a few months. It was overshadowed by Dota 2's largest esports event of the year; *The International*. While The International was the most watched esports event to that date, it did not last a whole season. In the same year, 2019, a record-breaking esports event took place; The League of Legends World Championship. That event had over 100 million viewers, cementing the game as the most viewed esport event of all time, clearly breaking every record. Within the same year, three different records were set, two of which were broken. This says a lot about the fast-paced growth within this industry.

One of the foremost reasons why the viewership of esports has been growing at such a high rate is the fact that not everyone knows about it; people are gradually learning and once they do, become addicted fanatics. The thing with normal sports is that they have always been around, kids are taught to play soccer and basketball ever since they learn how to walk or run for that matter. They have grown up playing these games in their schools, in organized leagues, and having different tournaments. However, esports has only begun to accept hockey stick in popularity even though it has been around for a while. Thus, it is natural for a lot of people to be unaware of it creating an extremely high ceiling for continued growth.

Our extreme social connectedness is advantageous for esports in this sense because it has made it easier for millions of people to learn about it and hop on the bandwagon. Back in 2015, there were just a little more than 800,000 people who had heard about esports. In just another year, the number reached over a billion people, and from there, they kept increasing by a couple hundred thousand every year. The awareness of esports had risen to 1.28 billion by 2017, then 1.43 billion by 2018, and an estimate of 1.57 billion in 2019. Alongside awareness, the viewership numbers have also skyrocketed, and consequently, the industry will see further revenue growth. Since we are talking about how massively these numbers have shot up, it brings us to this question; *who are these viewers?*

The Audience

According to statistics, the percentage of internet users who watch esports tournaments are as follows:

- 16-24-year-olds; 32%

- 25-24-year-olds; 30%

- 35-44-year-olds; 19%

- 45-54-year-olds; 10%

- 55-64-year-olds; 6%.

Popularity in Gen Z

To understand why Gen Z holds streaming in such high regards, we must understand how the fact that they are mobile natives changes their entire perception. When the oldest Gen Z member was just nine years old, the iPhone was released. This means that a world where unlimited information was more than a swipe or tap away is unknown. As social media is on the rise, they have thousands of friends worldwide, just a click away, ready to comment on and react to every part of their lives.

Due to this level of interconnectedness, and growing social media trends, the way Gen Z views the world is different from how older generations did. For instance, this has taught them to always think in terms of "influence," particularly the kind that exhibits itself in news feeds, likes and follows. Seven in ten teenagers say that they relate more to influencers than traditional celebrities, mainly because those so-called 'influencers' are just other normal people like them. There is nothing out of the ordinary about them. Therefore, taking this point in perspective, it only makes all the sense in the world that they are more drawn towards gaming stars: streamers, vloggers, and professional players – individuals just like them. Unlike traditional sports, almost everyone who watches esports actively plays the games that they watch. The gap between the players and the audience is actually very, very small.

Unlike a sport like basketball where the requirement for players like LeBron James are unusual height, speed, leaping ability and the fact that they are born with unheard of talents, esports players are just like the viewers themselves. They play on similar equipment, lead comparable lifestyles and play the exact same games. The primary differentiator is usually the lack of infrastructure. There is a social commentary argument to be made about the equal opportunity for access to high-speed internet and robust gaming consoles or computers. Otherwise, young gamers look at esports star athletes and they look just like them.

The fact of the matter is that esports is not just 'organized competitive video gaming.' It is the outcome of a much larger movement, one that is empowered by digital native Gen Z and Millennial consumers. Those who want to connect, share, and compete in new ways can do this in ways that you ordinarily cannot in traditional sports like football, baseball, or basketball. This could also be the reason these traditional sports' viewership has been declining or has reached a plateau. For example, 76% of esports fans have said that watching and playing esports is taking away from hours spent watching conventional sports. Back in 2018, the NFL, which was the only sport able to resist this negative trend, also faced a double-digit decline in the viewership of that season. Due to these changes in trends, both high-profile players and sports leagues have now started to take notice of esports and get in on the action.

Can esports become More Popular than Traditional Sports?

According to a study done by OverActive Media, in Ontario, Canada, it is on track to do just that. Millennials and Gen Z love to watch Fortnite and Overwatch matches just as much as the local traditional sports teams during season games. Charlton Insights surveyed with 1,457 people between the ages of 13-49 years. The results showed that Gen Z and Millennials are more likely to be gamers (69%)[6] than traditional sports fans (61%). According to NewZoo, in 2018,

---

[6]*Esports becoming as popular as regular sports with younger generations* Retrieved from

revenues from esports overtook and surpassed that of the WWE's. Esports has become well respected throughout the world, and even traditional sports outlets cover it now.

Are Women Interested in esports?

In 2016, women's viewership of esports was 23.9% of all watchers. By the fourth quarter of 2018, that number shot up to 30.4%. A study[7] conducted by an analyst firm Interpret, who surveyed 9000 US residents stated:

"If two years from now, the female audience grabs an additional 6.5% in share, esports viewership will be in gender parity with what we consider standard among traditional console and PC games."

The study took place over two years, where these people were surveyed once every quarter to ascertain how women's interaction with games was. Considering the substantial representation of men in professional athletes and esports audiences in the past, a 6.5% change is a huge leap. Further statistics show that:

- Of the people who play games considered an esports player on a console or PC, just 35% are female.

- Of those who regard themselves as esports watchers, 30% are women.

- Of those who watch esports leagues, 20% are women.

- Casual gaming, on the other hand, is dominated by women at 66%.

This slow increase in female esports fan base could be because mobile games have been prevailing at an increasing rate. At the end of the day, it all comes down to one thing; esports has captured a great audience and the community keeps growing exponentially. With the trends around the world evolving, brands will

---

https://www.dailyesports.gg/esports-becoming-as-popular-as-regular-sports-with-younger-generations/
[7]Female viewership of esports increasing Retrieved from
https://www.gamesindustry.biz/articles/2019-02-21-female-viewership-of-esports-increasing

be well advised to look at both men and women to reach via advertisements and sponsorships.

Chapter 4: The Xbox War

War. War never changes, especially when it comes to console wars. The console war between Sony PlayStation and Microsoft Xbox is not a new one. Truth be told, Sony was already deep into the video game industry before Microsoft, as they started way back in the late '80s. PlayStation was the reigning console system in the market. It has dominated since the mid-90s. The original PlayStation sold a few hundred million units, a staggering figure at the time.

By the late 1990s, Microsoft was concerned about the possibility of encroachment in the console market blending into the home PC, where Microsoft dominated

Therefore, Xbox had a bid to win back territory for Microsoft. While Xbox may have been the new kid on the block, all of Bill Gates empire forces were behind it. Before Xbox, Microsoft had already ported Windows CE to the Sega Dreamcast, giving them experience in the console market.

More importantly, they had some of the best programming teams on the planet. The long-term distribution plan for the Xbox was to own the living room. That led to ambitious missteps along the way. One of their original plans was too heavily focused on integrating it with other Microsoft products, such as DirectX technology. But their notion was correct, the fight truly is much more than just the console market. Sony and Microsoft look forward to the time of integration of various electronic devices within the home. Consoles are evolving for higher speed internet access, for playing music, and even for personal computing.

The Evolution of Xbox & PlayStation

The PlayStation brand was launched by Sony back in 1994. Since then, there have been four major consoles released by the company – all of which came with designs that had been refreshed. The PlayStation division is a representation of 78% of Sony's profits now.

Before the original Xbox was released in 2001, many doubted Microsoft's prospects of competing in the video game console business. Until that point, the company was primarily a PC software vendor, and there was no room for four major consoles. It also had to compete with PlayStation 2 and Nintendo GameCube at the time. Despite initial stiff competition and many pitfalls along the way, the Xbox brand has made significant progress over the last 15 years to become a household name in the hardware world and an essential pillar of Microsoft's business. It has since sold over 100 million consoles.

Play Station

The original PlayStation was launched on December 3, 1994, in Japan. It became the first video game console to ship more than 100 million units. It is considered part of the fifth-generation game console and competed against the Sega Saturn and Nintendo 64 in the mid-'90s. The console's catalyst originated from a failed partnership with Nintendo when Sony was in talks about creating an add-on for Super Nintendo.

The PlayStation featured a dual-speed CD-ROM drive, a single-core CPU, with 2MB of RAM with 1MB of video that delivered up to 360,000 polygons per second with graphics. The original PlayStation played a vital role in moving the industry from 2D graphics to real-time 3D rendering. Its use of the compact disc format allowed it to pursue high-fidelity full-motion video, something competing N64s struggled with their space-limited cartridges. PlayStation does not have an internal hard drive as they took a different approach to storage. Instead, the game required the use of memory cards, an average of 128KB in size. It is also notable that the PlayStation did not initially ship with the DualShock Controller. Instead, its original PlayStation controller lacked thumbsticks and force-response technology. Sony would later release its first DualShock controller in 1997, which would add these features.

PSOne

Sony released the PSOne on July 7, 2000. It was smaller, featuring a resigned chassis that was rounder and received an updated graphical user interface.

PlayStation 2

First released in Japan on March 4, 2000, the PlayStation 2 became the best-selling console ever, selling over 155 million units over 12 years. The PS2 is a part of the sixth generation of consoles and competed with the Sega Dreamcast, Nintendo's GameCube, and Microsoft's Xbox. The PS2's main leverage on the competition was the size of its sheer library - the console produced more than 2,000 games.

The PS2 launched with its Emotion Engine CPU, a single-core processor clocked at 294.9MHz. It had 32MB system RAM and 4MB video RAM - the console lagged behind most PS1 games, a rare feature at the time. It was also the first console to support DVDs - which, in addition to enabling games with large assets, allowed the PS2 to play DVD movies, thereby eliminating the need in the home for an additional, expensive stand-alone DVD player. Remember what we said about owning the living room. It was also the first console to support USB ports, which the PlayStation EyeToy camera would benefit from in the 2003 release.

While the original console allowed users to install an optional 40GB hard drive, it still used a memory card. Unlike the PS1, however, in which a 128 KB card was used, storage here was increased to 8 MB. The PS2 also introduced DualShock 2. While still wired, this controller showed a new black finish and tight stick.

Xbox

Microsoft made its original big, black, and green Xbox debut in North America on November 15, 2001. It was retailed for $300 and launched within a sixth-generation console, making it the first major gaming system built by an American company since the Attic Jaguar. Before the launch, Microsoft's major gaming efforts were focused on the PC, where its Windows operating system had a virtual monopoly on the market. The Washington based company based in Redmond, had a chance to launch the console when it developed a custom version of Windows CE for the Sega Dreamcast that supported a version of its DirectX API.

After seeing how Sony's console business was diverging from PC game sales and fearing that rival company PlayStation 2 would overtake the PC and thereby own the living room, Microsoft decided to release its system to directly compete. Microsoft engineers put together an early prototype as a side project using Dell laptop parts. Microsoft decided to invest and iterate on this design, which eventually paved the way for the Xbox to use the PC's x86 architecture, which was rare for a console. The operating system was based on the architectural kernel of Windows. The system was originally called the DirectX box, as it used the company's DirectX API, but was shortened to Xbox after focus groups liked that name better.

The console was equipped with a 32-bit Intel Celeron Pentium III hybrid CPU clocked at 733 MHz. It had a 64 MB DDR SDRAM installed at 200 MHz in a dual-channel configuration. For its GPU, Xbox used a custom chip from Nvidia based on the company's GeForce 3 line of graphics cards and was clocked at 233MHz. The GPU supported Microsoft's DirectX 8 API and was able to deliver 7.3 gigaflops of performance. Although it supported a 32MB memory card, it also came with an 8GB hard drive, which was a costly investment for the company. It became the first console to include a built-in HDD.

Developers generally agreed that the Xbox was more powerful than the competing games Cube and PlayStation 2, leading to some third-party ports to take advantage of the additional processing power. It ended up with sales of more than 24 million units, which more or less led to the end of Nintendo's systems. Although it came in the second generation and established a reputation for the company in the console space, it was sold at a disadvantage, and still fell far short of matching PS2 sales.

Despite significant efforts by Microsoft, the console struggled in Japan where Sony ruled, with some figures estimating that it had sold only about half a million systems. Compared to the competition, the Xbox became a haven for more western games and first-person shooters, the latter of which were relatively rare on consoles. Additionally, the Xbox was also the first console to support a broadband Ethernet port, further making way for Xbox Live.

PlayStation 2 Slimline

In September 2004, Sony continued its strategy of releasing smaller versions of its console when it unveiled the PlayStation 2 Slimline. Not only was the system small, but it was also quiet and included a built-in Ethernet port.

Xbox 360

Microsoft released its second console in North America on November 22, 2005, almost a year before its PlayStation 3 and Nintendo Wii competitors. The Xbox 360 came in two SKUs at launch. The high-end Pro version came with a 20GB hard drive and retailed for $400, but Microsoft also wanted to offer a cheaper model that hit the $ 300 price point and released the core model. This SKU lacked a hard drive, causing some confusion among game developers who were not initially sure how to design the game around this fragmented barrier. However, users were able to purchase and added an optional Xbox hard drive to the console.

The first version of the Xbox 360 was white, though you could swap the front face-plate to customize the aesthetics slightly.

Over its lifetime, Microsoft's second console significantly outperformed its initial effort and sold more than 84 million units worldwide. It remained weak in Japan, however, estimated again to have sold only about 1.5 million units. Despite struggling in the land of the rising sun, it remains Microsoft's best-selling system to date.

The Xbox 360 moved away from the x86 architecture that it used in the original console. Microsoft opted to go with the IBM PowerPC solution. Its triple-core, six-thread CPU was named Xenon and clocked at 3.2GHz. After a legal payment dispute with Nvidia over the original Xbox GPU, Microsoft decided to switch and go with ATI for its graphics. The 360 used a custom solution called Xenos based on the manufacturer's Radeon X1800 graphics card. For memory, the system used 512MB of shared GDDR3 RAM at 700MHz. Memory was a costly investment for Microsoft at the time, with the company teaming up with studios like Epic Games to properly run games like Gears of War. The console supported

DirectX 9, and developers generally considered the Xbox 360 easy to program than the PS3 with its complex cell processor. The result of multiplier games on the system was that they looked better on the Xbox 360.

Through software emulation, the console almost offered backward compatibility with the original Xbox library, although many ports suffered from glitches of varying severity.

The Xbox 360 eventually became a popular living room entertainment center. It supported stuttering streaming services like Netflix and allowed users to stream media from local PCs on the network. It supported the CD, DVD, and now-defunct HD DVD standard through an optional add-on accessory.

While the console was originally shipped with the Xbox 360 dashboard UI offering a tab-based "blade" interface, the system would eventually get multiple emulsions. The first major revision took place in 2008 and was called the New Xbox Experience (NXE). It was inspired by Microsoft's Windows Media Center and Zune design plans. This update also introduced the ability to install the game to reduce load time. The console received its second major UI update in 2011 when it was modeled after Microsoft's Windows 8 Metro design language. This update added cloud storage for games, Bing voice search, and more.

While the Xbox 360 became a huge success for Microsoft, the early models were plagued by what gamers would refer to as the Red Ring of Death, highlighting the fact that a red LED ring pointed to an overheating issue on the console would appear. This was a serious problem that was eventually going to destroy the system. Users ended up coming up with ridiculous improvements, including baking the console's motherboard in the oven. This prompted Microsoft to spend more than a billion dollars on extending the console's warranty by three years.

PlayStation 3

First released in Japan on November 11, 2006 (a week after its North American debut), the PlayStation 3 sold over 80 million units worldwide and competed with Microsoft's Xbox 360 and Nintendo Wii. (The Wii was an innovative offering that utilized wireless motion sensor technology and brought gaming to people of all ages.) Launching at $599.99, the PlayStation 3 was the most expensive system of the bunch, but it was the first console to feature a Blu-ray DVD drive and was priced at a cheaper price point than most stand-alone Blu-ray players when launched.

At the heart of the PS3 was its proprietary cell processor. Sony designed the chip in partnership with Toshiba and IBM. However, CPU became controversial among developers because of how difficult it was to program. The cell had seven cores and clocked at 3.2GHz. The PS3's graphics used Nvidia's RSX reality synthesizer GPU with 256 MB of VRAM and is clocked at 550 MHz. The PS3 was also the first PlayStation system to support HDMI and 1080p output. Early versions of the PS3 were backward compatible with PS2 games, but this was because Sony physically incorporated the PS2 processor inside the chassis. To cut costs, Sony later removed the feature shortly after launch.

PlayStation 3 also introduced Wi-Fi connectivity and it came with a 20GB internal hard drive. This allowed users to set up their HDDs. Additionally, the console also saw the birth of the PlayStation network, which allowed players to download games and use video-watching apps such as Netflix and YouTube. Additionally, the PS3 launched the company's PlayStation Plus subscription service, which gave gamers early access to the Beatus gaming and game discounts.

The PS3 also introduced DualShock 3, the first wireless version of Sony's long-lasting controller. On top of that, the DS3 also had motion-sensing technology. Following the success of the Nintendo Wii, Sony released its own PlayStation Move Controller for the PS3 in 2010.

The Xbox 360 Elite

Microsoft released Xbox 360 Elite in 2007. It was black and equipped with a larger 120GB hard drive, an HDMI output, and built-in Wi-Fi.

The Xbox 360 Arcade

Further down the lane, in October 2007, Microsoft released the Xbox 360 Arcade at an affordable price of $280 to replace the Core models. Like the Core units before it, the Arcade SKU did not have a hard drive, including a 256MB memory card. The most significant difference it had was the added HDMI port.

PlayStation 3 Slim

Sony released the PS3 Slim in September 2009. Not only was it about a third smaller and lighter, but as the cell moved to a new 45nm manufacturing process, it also consumed less power and ran cooler and quieter than the original model. Slim removed the power switch on the back of the console. The console also had a new PS3 logo, with Sony moving away from the original model's font (also famously featured in Toby Maguire's Spider-Man films).

Xbox 360 S

In 2010, Microsoft re-released the first Xbox 360. The Xbox 360S launched for $300 and came with a relatively large 250GB hard drive. It was also known as the slim model with its small, lightweight design and small power brick. It was also more angular and had a shiny black finish.

The S model used a more power-efficient processor and motherboard that minimized the original design's thermal issues that could lead to the "red ring of death." As a result, it was a much more stable operating system. The S model replaced physical power and eject buttons with touch-sensitive ones and offered 802.11n Wi-Fi support with two additional USB ports. When it was set vertically, it also moved the hard drive bay from the top of the chassis to the bottom.

Kinect

Microsoft released its Kinect add for the Xbox 360 on November 11, 2010, nearly five years after the console's launch. In addition to supporting voice commands, it was a motion control device that used relatively advanced sensors, which allow users to play games with their bodies instead of controllers.

This represented Microsoft's first major step in speed control and ended up being a financial hit. Despite being released relatively late in the console's lifecycle, Kinect became the fastest-selling consumer electronics device and sold eight million units within 60 days. To date, Microsoft has sold over 24 million first-generation Kinects, equaling it with sales of the original Xbox console.

The Kinect competed against the Nintendo Wii Remote and the PlayStation Move Controller.

PlayStation 3 Super Slim

The PlayStation 3 Super Slim, released in September 2012, marked the first time Sony made a second design revision for one of its mainline consoles. Here, Sony removed the front slot-loading disk tray. In its place, the chassis was redesigned to include a sliding lid covering the optical drive, which was to be accessed from above the console. Not only was the console slimmer than the previous model, but at 4.3 pounds, it was also three pounds lighter.

Xbox 360 E

Microsoft released its final 360 design in April 2013. The Xbox 360 E launched for $250 and included a 250GB hard drive. The console was slightly smaller and quieter than the Xbox S model and was designed for budget-conscious customers who weren't willing to spend $500 for the upcoming Xbox One. It was designed to look similar to the Xbox One with a mix of black matte and gloss finish.

The E model also marked the return of physical strength and the eviction button. The design eliminated the console's S / PDIF and legacy AV connectors, however, and re-connected users to HDMI-only video connections. The 360E version offered four USB ports, which was less than its earlier S model.

PlayStation 4

Sony released PlayStation 4 in North America in November 2013, and it sold over one million units on its first day, making it the fastest-selling console in 24 hours. The PS4 first released Sony as a CPU based console on the x86 instruction set, which is the same processor architecture that a gaming PC uses. In particular, it used an 8-core AMD x86-64 Jaguar CPU available at 1.6GHz with 8GB of GDDR5 memory, which it shares with its integrated AMD Radeon GPU. The PS4 also introduced the ability to upload and share gameplay clips. A share button was added to the DualShock 4 controller, which also received an ergonomic overhaul, and a headset and mic port were added.

Xbox One

Microsoft released the eighth-generation console in November 2013. Launched by Xbox One for $500, the company introduced it as the ultimate entertainment system and bundled every unit with a second-generation Kinect. The new Kinect used 1080p cameras that provide a wider angle, better tracking accuracy, and heart rate monitoring. While Microsoft initially claimed that the Kinect was an integral part of the experience and needed to be kept plugged in at all times, the company eventually offered a cheaper $400 SKU. They dropped the sensor requirement to be more competitive with Sony for the $400 PS4 console. Users also voiced privacy concerns on the camera. Is my gaming console spying on me? A familiar argument to this day with smart TV and devices. Microsoft started selling Kinect separately for $ 150.

Xbox One went back to PC's x86 instruction set. The console used AMD's custom Jaguar accelerated processing unit, which includes two quad-core modules at 1.75GHz. The system used AMD's Durango integrated graphics solution based on the company's Radeon HD 7000 series GPU. The Durango was clocked at 853MHz and is capable of delivering 1.31 teraflops of performance. For memory, the Xbox One used 8GB of shared DDR3 RAM shared at 2133MHz, but it also made the 32MB of ESRAM embedded on the APU faster. The console is generally considered slightly weaker than the competing PS4, which did not use any ESRAM but had 8GB of faster GDDR5 memory. Some third-party ports run at lower native resolution than Sony's systems.

Beginning in June 2015, the console offered backward compatibility with many Xbox 360 games through the software Xbox. In 2017, Microsoft announced that Xbox One would support original Xbox games as well.

The Xbox One removed the ability to swap hard drives but allowed users to use external USB 3.0 drives to increase storage. You could also play media from USB devices in addition to CD, DVD, and Blu-ray discs. In terms of network connectivity, the Xbox One had support for Gigabit Ethernet, 802.11n, and Wi-Fi Direct.

For its design, the Xbox One uses a two-tone chassis that mixes matte black with a glossy finish and brings back capacitive touch buttons. While the console is relatively large, it runs cooler and quieter than Sony's competitor PlayStation 4.

Piggybacking on the 360's success as a multimedia device, Microsoft heavily pushed the console's multimedia functionality and added the ability to record and stream gameplay. The original operating system ran a stripped-down version of Windows 8 that was based on the operating system's tile-based design language. The user interface initially received a lot of criticism for being unilateral. It received several updates over the years, and in 2016 it added Cortana voice support.

Microsoft keeps Xbox One sales numbers close to the vest, but the industry estimates it to have had about 26 million units sold as of January 2017. It is still behind Sony's PS4, which has shipped over 60 million consoles to date.

PlayStation 4 Slim

The PS4 Slim continued the tradition of releasing smaller, lighter variants of Sony - and this console did away with the sharp edges of the PS4 in favor of rounded corners. Some upgrades under the hood included 5GHz Wi-Fi, Bluetooth 4.0, and USB 3.1 support. The system was also more efficient and slightly cooler, and quieter than the original model. One major drawback? They removed the popular PS4's S / PDIF optical port.

Xbox One S

Microsoft released its Xbox One S version in August 2016. The console redesign was about 40 percent smaller than the previous model and integrated the power supply unit into the chassis. It comes in a predominantly matte white aesthetic with black accents.

The One S once again returned physical power and eject buttons and added 4K Blu-ray drives with high-dynamic-range (HDR) support. The console's GPU was more powerful, going from 853MHz to 914MHz. The higher frequency was added to compensate for the additional processing overhead that HDR introduces. The Xbox One S also upscaled 4K to games. The console offered three hard drive sizes: 500GB, 1TB, and 2TB, which cost $ 299, $349, and $ 399, respectively. While the Xbox One S made many improvements to the base model, it removed the Kinect port. Microsoft offered a free Kinect adapter for a limited time, but they eventually decided to sell it separately.

Xbox One X

The Xbox One X was released with great fanfare in 2017 with a $500 MSRP. Microsoft pitched the One X as a 4K-capable console that delivered six teraflops of performance but still played games and software comparable to existing Xbox One systems. The One X still used an 8-core AMD system-on-a-chip like its predecessor but was heavily tweaked and extended to 2.3 GHz. It also used 12GB of shared GDDR5 RAM. Its GPU used a Radeon solution equipped with 40 compute units based on AMD's Polaris micro-architecture and clocked at 1172MHz.

The console is backward compatible with the Xbox. In terms of design, the Xbox One X is the company's smallest console. Aesthetically, it looks like the Black Xbox One S. Although the console is geared toward 4K enthusiasts with a UHD HDR-capable Blu-ray player and its high-end specs, Microsoft claims the Xbox One X will enable gaming for those who want ultra-high-definition. The system supported anisotropic filtering, reduce the load time, and make 1080p HD gameplay faster than standard HD output.

PlayStation 4 Pro

The PS4 Pro came out in November 2016. Unlike the traditional design refresh, the PS4 Pro offered a notable bump in specs. The console was based on

AMD's Polaris graphics and had 4.2 teraflops of GPU performance, more than double the PS4 1.84 of the original performance. Also, the Pro supported 4K gaming capabilities. The console was fully backward compatible with the PS4, and developers used additional processing power to increase the graphical fidelity of existing titles at 1080p.

To Sum It Up... Xbox One vs. PS4

The war between Microsoft's Xbox and Sony's PlayStation is not new. As you can see, it has been ongoing for decades now. Over the years, they released one gaming console after another in hopes of leaving their competitor behind. Both systems are in fierce competition with one another and have pretty distinct differences. True gaming aficionados will appreciate a side-by-side comparison.

Performance

Both systems can play the same games. However, performance is dependent on the console you are using. The slim PS4 is a more powerful machine with a slightly greater ability to display games at a higher resolution than usual. The difference is not always drastic, but on most TVs, PS4 titles will simply look better. There are some claims of PS4 dropping frames on some games, and while this has not been reported as a widespread issue - many games run at 30 or 60 frames per second without issue - it's still worth noting is.

The best course of action is to see how your favorite game performs before you make a decision. Many gaming websites upload side-by-side graphics comparisons for major releases, allowing you to get an idea of what to expect. If you are investing in a more expensive PlayStation 4 Pro or Xbox One X console, however, Microsoft gains. The Xbox One X is capable of playing many games at native 4K resolution and consistently outperforms Sony's premium console.

In any case, these differences only apply to third-party games, where both versions can be compared side-by-side. First-party titles tend to take better advantage of the system they're developed for, and that's why it would be nice.

Controller

The standard Xbox One controller retains many of the main elements of the 360 controllers. It also adds two more rumble motors and loses the heavy battery pack on the rear. There are also small thumb pads on analog sticks, some of which will be refreshed, others disappointing. Microsoft also released an "elite" version of its controller, which allows for multiple customization options and multiple triggers for various customization options. While the Elite controller is undoubtedly exciting, it also costs $ 150. Unless you are the hardest of hardcore, you would not need anything.

The DualShock 4, on the other hand, shows wider improvements across the board than previous DualShock controllers. It is large and outfitted with outward-curving triggers, plus a clickable touchpad on the front and multifunctional lightbar. The controller also has a little speaker, which some games use very effectively. The embedded thumb pads are larger than the Xbox controller, although this only corresponds to the controller. Overall, the PS4 controller feels a bit harder and will fit the hands of most gamers better. It is a slim margin of victory, but still a win.

Ports and Storage

Ports are a notable difference between an Xbox and PS4. Microsoft packaged an IR blaster and two HDMI inputs into one so that you can connect the console to the satellite box and cable TV. With Sony abandoning these ports, it is clear that Microsoft wants to win over a wider consumer demographic. Both consoles tout an Ethernet port and two USB inputs, but only the PS4 comes with a camera port at this point. If you want to use Kinect on your Xbox One S or X, you'll need an adapter that is now out of production.

Both consoles are available with 500GB or 1TB of storage space, enough to house a decent collection of games and other media. Still, 1TB of storage is the bare minimum for most desktop PCs, and around four years into the life cycle of these consoles, space can be at a premium if you're regularly downloading new games. Fortunately, the storage of both systems can be easily expanded through external hard drives.

Overall, the Xbox One and PS4 have to be slightly different in terms of connectivity and storage. The wide selection of ports gives the Xbox a win.

Game selection

Both the Xbox One and PS4 have libraries with hundreds of games, and each console has its own set of exclusions. In many ways, this is one of the major selling points for choosing one console over the other. Although most third-party games are available on both systems, there are exceptions. Both Microsoft and Sony deal to secure console exclusives now and then (though most Microsoft games are also available on PCs these days).

If you want to get a console for your exclusives, you might want to get PlayStation 4. Sony's first-party studio releases several great exclusives for the system each year, such as God of War, Marvel's Spider-Man. And MLB: Show Series, and its third-party partners also develop adjectives such as Detroit: Being Human and Nioh.

Meanwhile, Xbox One has some notable games every year. Apart from the big series like Forza, Halo, and Gears of War, the exclusives we've seen for Exclusive Xbox One are minimal. There are some exceptions, such as Sunset Overdrive and the inventive pirate game Sea of Thieves, but pale compared to what Sony offers to its players.

See further, PS4 has Ghost of Tsushima, Dreams, and The Last of Us Part II. Microsoft has Halo Infiniti, Orient and the Wise of the Wisps, and possible Gears of War tactics as it turns down console generation; things seem to be out in the evening. Still, the PS4 has a vast back catalog of exclusives that offer offerings on Xbox Destroys. One.

Most of the time, unless you are a die-hard fan of a specific franchise or one in particular that catches your eye, you will be able to play the biggest game on either console. The gamer games such as The Witcher 3 and Fallout 4 are available on both systems. But if you have to choose one for the game alone, it is an easy decision.

Backward Compatibility

As happened with the Xbox 360, the Xbox One provides backward compatibility for a selected number of games, although the number has grown significantly since the feature launched in 2015. If you insert Xbox 360 games into Xbox One, you may be able to download a digital version of the said title. Some games are also available to purchase through Microsoft's digital store, and some games come with free digital copies of older Xbox 360 games (i.e., Fallout 4). They are not everything; Every month, Xbox Live Gold members will receive a free Xbox 360 game as part of Microsoft's Games with Gold program.

When it comes to playing older games on the PS4, you currently have only one option: PlayStation Now. PSNow is a streaming service that allows you to play PS3 games (and some older PS4 titles) for $ 20 a month or $ 45 for three months. Unfortunately, depending on your internet speed, the game performance may be slowed due to lag. The catalog is not comprehensive either, and even if you own a physical or digital copy of an old game, you will have to pay to play it. It was rumored that Sony had planned to bring some PS1 and PS2 classics to the PSNow twist, but that is yet to happen. Simply put, you cannot insert an old PS disc into your PS4 and play it. If you need to scratch the retro PlayStation itch, you probably want to keep those old consoles around.

Online services

Sony and Microsoft offer similar online services. Sony's PlayStation Plus and Microsoft's Xbox Live Gold offer users online gaming, free monthly games, discounts, and other special features for an annual fee. Both services clock $ 10 per month or $ 60 for a year. The Xbox Play Anywhere initiative, which includes select titles, allows gamers to play the game on their Xbox One and their Windows 10 PCs.

PS4 users have some advantages of their own; PlayStation Now, as noted above, allows gamers to stream a light of their PS4 to PS3 titles. If you want the game to run smoothly, it is an excellent service, although you need a good internet connection.

A key feature is to hit the scales in favor of PlayStation, though - free games. Both PlayStations Plus and Xbox Live Gold subscribers earn free games monthly, but over the years, PlayStation selections have proven to be better. Partly due to the PS4's improved exclusive title selection. Sony has introduced some of the best games of this console generation, like Bloodborne, for free.

Peripherals

Kinect was a useful launch peripheral for the Xbox One, but Microsoft has discontinued the motion-sensing camera, leaving new Xbox One players not finding a good way to capture their faces if they wanted to live stream the game Huh. On the other hand, the PlayStation camera is a less robust device, but it is still being produced and works well - you can also use it to sign in to your profile. Xbox gamers in possession of an Oculus Rift VR can stream any Xbox One game to an Oculus headset and select one of three immersive VR environments: "Citadel," "Retreat," and "Dome." This is a very nice feature that allows players to play games in IMAX mainly but does not have additional rift functionality. On the other hand, we were blown away when Sony's PSVR was released, and as the list of compatible games grew, so did the value of VR. You will need a PlayStation camera; If you don't already have one, you can bundle it with a PSVR and a game for about $ 300.

In any case, the PSVR is surprisingly sophisticated and extremely fun. A cool "social screen" feature feeds the display from the headset on your TV, so people can see what you're watching. The PSVR-compatible game is designed with the experience in mind, so it's more than just a giant screen. Some games work better than others, but this is precisely the experience most PlayStation gamers want.

User Interface

The PS4's interface is designed to be accessible. It is simple, and anyone can detect it. While it can often get crowded when building your library, you can sort games in a custom folder to reduce the burden of scrolling.

The UI of the Xbox One is somewhat more complicated but also more robust and functional. The interface is designed to work similarly to Windows 10, and although it may take some time to pronounce correctly, the design is far more accessible and intuitive once you've done it. Microsoft also regularly updates the Xbox One interface, adding features at the behest of the gaming community. While the PS4's menu is simple to navigate for newbies, the Xbox has more features to help you discover the games or apps you're searching for.

Media Interface and Apps

Both the PS4 and Xbox One were built with gaming in mind only. Microsoft has spoken time and time again about its bold vision for its world, where the Xbox One is the only box in your living room, and believe it or not, the person is quickly achieving that vision. The One is now equal parts streaming box and gaming console, and unlike Sony's next-gen counterpart, the system is designed to operate your cable box and record regular programming.

Both consoles have common third-party subscription services such as Netflix and Amazon Instant Video and app offerings such as Hulu Plus, HBO Go, Twitch, Ustream, and Crackle. While there was a long period where the Xbox Store offered far more apps than its PlayStation counterpart, which has mostly been removed, and few - if any - apps you can't find on both consoles.

The Xbox naturally compresses PCM audio data, while the PS4 supports DTS HD; There is little difference (if any) in terms of audio quality. A recent update added bitstream pass-through support for the Xbox One, allowing connected AV receivers to now decode audio natively. This means that newer, object-based audio formats such as Dolby Atmos and DTS: X are supported via Blu-ray Disc audio, while PlayStation 4 has always supported bitstream pass-throughs.

Streaming

The PS3 was - and remains - an excellent media device capable of streaming music and video from your PC and playing directly from a USB-connected device. The PS4 took a while to grow to its capacity, but today it qualifies as a fully streaming console. Sony's PlayStation Now service offers over 100 PlayStation games for instant streaming, so unless you opt for a $ 20 or $ 45 subscription.

Microsoft has adopted a different approach to media streaming. The company optimized the Xbox One as a media device when it downgraded the Xbox Live paywall, giving users free access to Netflix (for apps like Netflix, yet you'll need a subscription to that particular service) Will. If you are a cable TV subscriber, you can connect your cable to the console for more functionality and performance. Previously, we crowned the Xbox winner here due to its cable integration, but the introduction of PS Now is also imminent. When the project xCloud officially launches at a later date, that may change.

While there is no denying the fact that both consoles offer a lot in their own ways, Sony's PlayStation 4 undoubtedly has the edge over the Xbox One. While the Xbox One is better for applications and content that is non-gaming related, if gaming is what you care about, Sony has built a dedicated gaming machine.

PlayStation and Xbox are making very different bets on the future of game

At the end of 2020, both Sony and Microsoft released major new consoles. Product constraints created buying frenzies and high demand. Sony PlayStation 5 and Microsoft Xbox Series S/X are new versions of the popular gaming consoles. Since 2013, the PlayStation 4 has sold a remarkable 100+ Million units. By comparison, Microsoft's last-generation console Xbox One, moved less than 50 Million units. According to industry experts, there are a number of reasons that the PlayStation 4 was able to score a 2 to 1 sales advantage over Xbox One.

POSITIONING – Sony treated its console as exclusively a niche gaming device, whereas Microsoft had aspirations for Xbox to "take over the living room".

DIGITAL RIGHTS MANAGEMENT (DRM) – When a game is downloaded, it is locked to the console where it was downloaded. Microsoft tried this with its physical game discs, an unpopular move that it later reversed.

EXCLUSIVE PARTNERSHIPS – Because Sony was focused on solely being a gaming console, it invested in exclusive titles for the PS4. Conversely, Microsoft added functionality such as its motion sensor Kinect camera, which raised the price.

As we fast forward to the future, the gaming strategies are diverging. Sony has followed a go-to market approach that a company such as Gillette takes with razors and blades. In this case, the razor (PlayStation 4 console and the new PlayStation 5 console) and blades (exclusive games and online services) is a tried and true strategy.

This model means that the "razor" (hardware) is usually a loss leader for the highly profitable "blades." Microsoft is diverting away from the loss-leading hardware and is transitioning to a service (SaaS – software as a service) model. By introducing Game Pass, a cloud gaming subscription with a recurring monthly fee, it expands the gaming reach beyond the Xbox to mobile devices as well. This is the identical shift that Microsoft made with its popular Windows license-based software when it moved to a cloud-based business based on recurring services revenue.

Chapter 5: Popular Games of Today

If there is one thing we know by now, it's that Gen Z loves gaming. As the gaming consoles continue to progress and the PlayStation 5 and Xbox Series X/S continuing to raise the bar on performance, game developers have to continue to develop new and innovative ideas to keep pace. The popular games around two decades ago are not as popular today, and what's popular today may not be in even the three to five years. Markets change, people's needs and interests change, and everyone loves the hot new thing. Let us explore a few of the popular games of today.

Fortnite

Fortnite[8] is the most famous battle royale game in the world. It was developed and published by Epic Games. Fortnite Battle Royale was released for the first time in 2017 for PlayStation 4, Xbox One, macOS, and Microsoft Windows. A year later, it was also released for iOS, Android, and Nintendo Switch. In the game, 100 players skydive onto an island, look for the best weapons and armor, defending themselves from other players, and killing others to be the last man or team standing.

There are different ways to play the game; players can fight alone (Solo), alongside one other player (Duo), or with a group of three other people (Squads). With the progression of the match, the island slowly starts to constrict, so the players not only have to defend themselves but also ensure they stay in the safe-zone.

The biggest distinctive feature of this game that sets it apart from others of the same genre is that it allows players to have construction elements. The players can do different things like building walls, obstacles, getting a strategic view advantage, or even covering incoming fire. The game takes a seasonal

---

[8] *Battle Royale: Everything you need to know* Retrieved from
https://www.tomsguide.com/us/fortnite-battle-royale-faq.news-25928.html

approach – each new season comes with new character customization content in the game, limited-time events.

Game Play

The main gameplay[9] for Fortnite Battle Royal follows the standard format for the Battle Royal genre. The game is usually played with each player or a squad of two to four players, with 100 players participating in each round. The round begins with players skydiving from weaponless, floating buses ("Battle Buses") and then deploying a glider over an area of land.

The island's fixed-layout includes several sites and locations (named in a figurative style, such as "Lazy Lake," "Pleasant Park," and "Retail Row"), which are mostly ghost cities during matches, while weapons use random distribution. Shields and other combat support facilities can be found by searching buildings and other sites.

The goal is to survive the last player or team by eliminating or avoiding other players. When playing in single mode, players are immediately terminated once they have exhausted their health. In squad mode, though, downed players can crawl around while bleeding; They can be eliminated immediately by an opponent or revived by a squadmate to help them. Initially, the expired players were left out of the match when the game was launched. In subsequent versions, the squadmates can attempt to revive a dropped player in various "reboot vans" scattered around the map, which are few and far between and open and players are at risk. Over time, the game's safe zone (representing the eye of the storm), decreases in size, and players caught outside the area will take damage. It directs the surviving players into tight spots, which the player faces. Supply drops rotate in random locations during a match, providing random weapons and items. Like the original Fortnite game, Fortnite Battle Royal is played primarily from a third-person perspective.

The primary difference from the other Battle Royal games to the Fortnite Battle Royale is the build system, which originated from the original Fortnite survival game. Almost everything in the environment can be destroyed and cut

---

[9] - *How to play Fortnite* Retrieved from https://www.gamesradar.com/how-to-play-fortnite/

to materials (wood, stone, and metal), which can then be used to build limited durabilities, such as walls, ramps, floors, and roofs, which can be used to your advantage in gameplay. These helps move the map, protect the player from bullets, or slow the progress of other players. Weak pieces can be destroyed in a few hits but can be built quickly, while stronger pieces can withstand more punishment, but take longer to build.

The game also revolves around players finishing their opponents for the final standing.

The game is free-to-play, supported by Microtransports, which allows players to purchase the game's internal currency, "Winderbucks," "V-Bucks." The V-Bucks are also shared with the main Fortnite: Save the World game, which offers players the opportunity to earn V-Bucks by completing missions or daily quests. The V-Bucks can then be used for cosmetic improvements to the player (character, pickaxe, glider skin, back-wear, and emotion). The game is run in chapters with multiple seasons, each season lasting approximately ten weeks. Each season features a special set of cosmetic items that can be obtained. These are offered through dual-track battle passes, which have a variety of tiers that allow players to gain experience by accomplishing the game's objectives and receive cosmetic rewards or other items in the process. Each player has access to the "Free" track of the Battle Pass, which offers fewer cosmetics that can be earned by cleaning multiple levels, while the player also passes the "Premium" track with the V-Bucks can purchase. This ultimately presents more challenges, and every tier player grants for advance. Players can use the V-Bucks to purchase tiers as well as a one-time Battle Pass.

Since its release, Epic Games has added new weapons and items and new features such as shopping vehicles and golf carts. Epic can deploy hotfixes to the game to accommodate aspects such as weapon characteristics and distribution, allowing them or players to discover important issues or glitches if necessary. It should also help in removing the items obtained from a process known as "vaulting." With the release of the standalone Fortnite Creative Gameplay mode in December 2018, a region of the Fortnite Battle Royale map called "The Block" featured a rotating selection of user-created creations developed in Creative Mode and approved by Epic.

A "Battle Lab" mode was added in December 2019 for players to create their own custom Battle Royal game. In 2020, a new "Party Royale" mode was added, placing it on a small map where combat and construction were disabled. Although non-lethal gameplay items, like paint guns and vehicles, were required, the map was intended to be used as a social space and hosting sports events such as concerts.

Before 2019, there was no special matchmaking at Fortnite, outside of platforms and regional boundaries. The game introduced skill-based matchmaking, based on an internal matrix that judges a player's skills in the game.

League of Legends

League of Legends[10], developed by Riot Games, is an online multiplayer battle arena genre video game. Initially, it was designed to run on the Microsoft Windows operating system. It was released in October 2009. Today, not only is it one of the most popular video games globally, but it is also the most popular esport, with over 100 million active users monthly. The game is readily available to be downloaded on Apple Macs and Windows PCs and is free to play.

League of Legends gameplay
General

In each game, there are two teams that consist of five members each. Each team starts the game on opposite sides of a map, near something called a "Nexus." For a team to win the match, they have to destroy the opposite team's Nexus. It's not as easy as it sounds. To destroy the opposing team's Nexus, each team has to work through 'turrets' (a series of towers) that have been placed alongside three paths to every base. Each player gains power along the way by accomplishing game objectives – this helps them earn experience points and gold, which can be used to increase the level of that player and buy powerful items. Ultimately that helps them get an advantage over their opponents.

---

[10]*What is League of Legends?* Retrieved from
https://www.riftherald.com/2016/9/29/13027318/lol-guide-how-to-watch-play-intro

Matchmaking

League of Legends is a season-based game. Matchmaking occurs based on the average Elo rating of each player. There are four different modes the game can currently be played in Normal, Co-op vs. AI, Custom, or Rank.

- In *a typical game*, the server tries to match players of equal skill level. It is possible to enter a systematic team of players, in which case the organized team is considered more potent than the individual players.

- A *co-op game* requires you to team up with four randomly selected players so that five versus five matches can be played against a team of five randomly selected bots.

- *The custom game* allows players to create a session and set its properties or join an existing session. Unlike the Co-op, Custom allows you to create teams of any category from one to five. Empty spaces can be filled by bots or players or can be empty.

- Ranked games are competitive matches open only to players who have reached the highest level; 30. It features a draft mode champion selection process, where a handful of champions are restricted before choosing.

Game Modes & Maps

There are different game modes: Classic and ARAM. The classic game mode is a base defense in which one slowly attempts to fight his way through confrontations and blockers with the help of the Nexus of opponents. The ARAM game mode (All Random All Mid) is a mode where the base defense is similar to the classic game mode but is located on a smaller, one path map. Maps are also called the "field of justice" in the *League of Legends*.

Classic

Summoner's Rift resembles the Defense of Ancients map with three lanes and supports up to five players per side. The maps put the two teams against a certain number of players; each team has its base, with re-spawn points, item shops, and

Nexus. Lanes connect the two bases. Periodically, minute waves emanate from the Nexus. Minions are AI-controlled NPCs that slash down the streets, killing any enemy they encounter. The lanes are lined with bastions that engage enemies within range. Once a turret is destroyed, it will not react. A newer element in the League of Legends is the blocker. Each lane has a blocker at both ends. If a team destroys an enemy blocker, more powerful 'super minions' will spread to that side. Unlike the turret, the inhibitors react after a few minutes.

In addition to the lanes, the map also includes "jungle" areas, populated with neutral monster camps. A champion for gold and experience can kill these monsters. Some of the larger monsters will provide the Assassin with a buffer, such as killing the Blue Sentinel gives his Assassin an Insight Buffer's Insight ability that helps them in battle. Another unique terrain feature is the brush. A brush blocks the unit's line of sight, allowing the champion to hide and set off a surprise attack or "gank." Each team's goal is to destroy the enemy Nexus, the winner being the one who manages to do it first. Surrender is possible through the voting system.

All Random All Mid

The Howling Abyss is only available for ARAM. It has similar gameplay with classic maps where players must destroy the Nexus to win here with some changes. Like classic maps, ARAM has only one lane and no jungle, again Spawn Point will not restore health or mana, and players cannot purchase items after passing the Nexus. Players must die to purchase the item again. ARAM features Health Relics due to the lack of health and mana restoration from the point of re-spawn. Players will start on level three, with gold and gold income, base XP generation, decreased re-spawn time, and a map-wide aura that increases mind regeneration, provides base armor / magic penetration, and lessens healing, alongside other changes make it a different, faster-paced game. Some items have been added, removed, and changed to fit the model.

Teamfight Tactics

This is an 8-player drafting tactics game that is free for all. It is available through the League Client but can even be found on mobile platforms. In that version, the player can recruit powerful champions, deploy them, and fight to become the last player. It does not only have a self-contained tab of the client but also a selection of different modes.

Champions

Every player has control over a single champion. When the game came out, there were only 40 champions. Today there are over 150 different champions available in the game, each of them having distinguishing characteristics. To give a brief description of their play style, every champion is tagged with specific attributes like 'tank,' 'fighter,' 'support.' Although some champions are more viable than others, they each have more than one attribute and can be played differently. When the battle begins, each player has to choose a champion to fight with during the battle. Depending on what the other player has unlocked, the choice of champions can be limited. Every week there are 14 champions made free temporarily so that players can try playing with them without unlocking them. This is called free champion rotation.

Champions gain experience through killing minions, champions, neutral monsters, or structures. Once they have reached a certain amount of experience, they level up. Every time the champion levels up, it increases their stats and adds an ability point that can later be spent to improve one of their four different abilities. Typically, every champion has three basic abilities that they can learn at any given time.

NBA 2K

When EA Sports (a division of Electronic Arts and publisher of Madden NFL, FIFA, and NHL games) refused to publish its sports franchises on Sega Dreamcast, Visual Concepts created a basketball franchise called NBA 2K. A simulation approach was taken by the series instead of the arcade-style prevalent in most basketball games. This game is recognized especially because of how life-like its details are – not just to the players, but even the arenas. After Sega stopped supporting Dreamcast, the series ended up becoming a multiplatform franchise under 2K Sports.

Gameplay

Each installment in the NBA 2K series emulates the National Basketball Association and introduces improvements over previous installments. In this way, the gameplay simulates a specific game of basketball. The player controls the entire team or a selected player. Objectives coincide with basketball and presentation rules that resemble real NBA games. Various game modes are depicted in the series, allowing for gameplay diversity. Many elements of the games have customizable options. Each game features teams and players from the current NBA season. Historical NBA teams and players are also depicted, as are Euro League teams and (starting with NBA 2K20) WNBA teams. Fantasy players and teams can also be created and compiled.

A key part of the series is its career mode, which is described as a game-themed role-playing video game. ESPN was the first game to feature an NBA basketball series, but it was not until NBA 2K10 and its successors that this mode became a more integral part of the series. The mode was initially titled 24/7 before converting to MyPlayer and settling on MyCareer. The mode centers on the player's basketball career created by the player; The player adapts to many aspects of his player and plays through his career in the NBA. Some major events of the player's career are depicted, such as the draft and retirement ceremony. A story often exists in the mode, and high school and college-level basketball is also depicted. Players upgrade their player's characteristics as they play and can participate in off-court activities.

Another mainstay of the series is a mode that allows the player to take control of the NBA franchise, acting as general manager. The mode has been featured in many NBA 2K games and is often titled Associations. The most recent games of the series include MyGM and MyLeague Mode. In mode, the player controls almost all aspects of the team, rather than playing the game with the team. As the player simulates through the season, they must meet the needs of the personnel and owner of the team.

MyTeam mode, which was introduced in NBA 2K13, focuses on building a team of players and competing online against other players' teams. The primary place for a player to receive players for their team is the card pack. The player buys a card pack that uses random items for the players, including the players. In addition to compiling a select group of players, players can also customize their team's jersey and court, among other things. The game mode went even further on NBA 2K19, with a MyTeam tournament among the best Xbox and PS4 players for the $250,000 prize. The series also featured other online-focused modes, such as Pro-Am, which focused on building a team with its custom players.

In addition to regulated NBA games, street basketball has been featured in several games in the series. Created players and real players can be used in such modes; Besides, some celebrities have made appearances as playable characters in the series. In recent games, the street basketball mode is titled Blacktop and MyPark. The blacktop is structured in a distinctive style of street basketball. MyPark has an open field full of players who can join different sports in different courts. Many games in the series have a mode that allows the player to organize a slam dunk contest.

The NBA has embraced this game and has actually created its own NBA 2K League, which is a joint venture between the National Basketball Association and Take-Two Interactive. The league launched in 2017 with over half of the NBA franchises also running a 2K team. Jonathan Sumers, who is the Director of Esports for the Cleveland Cavaliers NBA 2K team, shared that his favorite esports moment occurred the first time he went to an in-person competition at a sold-out Barclays Center in Brooklyn. With over 20,000 fans standing the cheering the entire time, he said, "I didn't expect the level of excitement and engagement that I witnessed. I walked away from the event realizing that esports is here to stay and will only get bigger."

Call of Duty

Call of Duty is one of those games that you would have to be an alien to not know about. It is a first-person shooter video game franchise that Activision published. It started back in 2003 when the scene of the games was set in World War II. As time passed, the games of this series have been set amid futuristic wars, the Cold War, and even outer space. It is quite literally one of the most successful franchises of all time. There are many different versions of the game, each compatible with one operating system or another – whether it's PC or an Xbox.

Call of Duty: Modern Warfare

The latest version of this game was released in 2019, and a new one usually scheduled to be released on a regular basis. It is a first-person shooter video game that Infinity Ward developed and Activision published. This is the sixteenth overall installment of the Call of Duty series and was released in October 2019, for PlayStation 5, Microsoft Windows, and Xbox One. The setting of the game is quite modern and realistic. In the campaign, a CIA officer follows alongside British SAS forces as they team up with rebels from Urzikistan, a fictional country. Together they combat against Russian forces who have invaded the country. The game has a Special Ops mode in which cooperative play missions are featured. This mode follows the campaign's story.

Gameplay

Modern Warfare's single-player campaign focuses on realism and consists of ethically based moral choices. In this, the player is evaluated and assigned a score at the end of each level. The players quickly discover whether the NPC is a threat, such as a civilian woman believed to be reaching for a gun, but then simply grabbing her child from a cradle. This collateral damage score is referred to as a hazard assessment. It is based on how many players injure or award from ranks A to F and are introduced to those who score higher. The character dialog will be different depending on the choices the player makes in the game.

The game's multiplayer has been modified to allow for a more tactical gameplay style, focusing on map exploration, door breeching, and the hardcore "realism" mode, which removes HUD. The mini-map was originally removed in favor of a compass-style marker, with friend signs and visual cues to detect opponents. Following a response from multiplayer beta testing, Infinity Ward re-enacted the mini-map but removed red dots representing enemy players (except for UAV Killstreak). Multiplayer facilitates Killstreaks' return (award based on kills), with the most recent Call of Duty titles being used, instead of using Scorestreaks (award based on score). However, assassins can be converted into Scorestreaks with the use of an in-game perk called "Pointman."

The online mode allows for a larger range of players within a map than in previous installments, with a new mode, "ground war" consisting of over 100 players, while there is another new mode, "Gunfight." Two teams of two players work against each other in short matches lasting forty seconds per round. The game includes an extensive weapon customization system, offering guns with a maximum of 60 attachments to choose from (which can be equipped at any one time). The introduction has also been given a facelift at the beginning of multiplayer matches. Although players in previous titles will remain motionless on the map as a timer will countdown to zero, players will be taken to the battle zone as part of various animations.

Modern Warfare is the first game in the series that did not feature Call of Duty: Ghosts as a zombie mode, instead featuring the cooperative "Special Ops" mode that previously existed in Call of Duty: Modern Warfare 2 and Call of Duty: Modern Warfare 3. Space Ops shared its narrative with both campaign and multiplayer. It includes a "Survival" mode, which is the special time for the release of PlayStation 4 in October 2020. At launch, Special Ops included four operations, multi-purpose missions requiring mandatory 4-player collaboration in a large open map. Also, Classic Special Ops, which feature small-scale missions similar to the original Space Ops mode.

The game also includes a Battle Royale game mode called Call of Duty: Warzone. The mode has 150 players battling teams of four, three, or singles. Call of Duty: Warzone has been released as a free standalone game that can be freely downloaded. The map features multiple locations prominently in multiplayer and special ops modes. Weapon modding is maintained with multiplayer mode, except for high headshot damage to reward targeting.

Warzone features looting as a core aspect, just like other Battle Royale games. Still, weapon customization is limited because players can only pick up weapon variants with a preset, unwanted attachment. Loot is simplified compared to other Battle Royal games in general, including Call of Duty: Black Ops 4's Blackout Mode: Instead of browsing through an inventory, players can see all of the looted items on the map for the taking.

Players can use armor plates to increase damage protection, and at any point, can carry up to five armor plates for swap and repair. When the players are defeated, instead of dying, they end up back at the "gulag" – a prison arena where defeated players can fight in one versus one scenario to score another chance to return to the main map. Players can also loot and stock cash, which is used to buy stations for killers, equipment, and revived tokens for downturned teammates.

Madden NFL

EA Tiburon developed a game based on the National Football League, called Madden NFL. A new version is published every season. Electronic Arts published the game. For 2020, NFL Madden 20 became the latest version of the long-running Madden NFL series and was released for PlayStation 4, Microsoft Windows, and Xbox One on August 2, 2019. The game features quarterback Patrick Mahomes from Kansas City Chief as the cover athlete. There is usually excitement each year as to who will be the featured NFL athlete that will grace that year's Madden cover.

Gameplay

Madden NFL 20 has a new "personalized career campaign," known as QB 1, being drawn by an NFL team, following a trip to a player-produced college quarterback from their participation in the College Football Playoff. In this mode, there are ten licensed college teams (Clemson, Florida State, Miami, Florida, LSU, Oregon, USC, Texas, Oklahoma, and Texas Tech) from the ACC, Big 12, Pac-12, and SEC available. The mode serves as an updated version of "Superstar Mode," where the player will take their custom player and control them throughout the career.

In September 2019, EA Sports launched another genre called Superstar KO as part of the game's first "season." Each team plays a touchdown and a drive from their own 25-yard line to make a two-point conversion in each round. If teams draw, the round is decided on a "tug-of-war," where each team makes three plays, and the team that advances wins the round. After each round, the winner can draft a player from the rival team.

EA continued including accessibility features for blind and visually impaired end users. Not the least of which is the menu narration, in which the options are played using a synthesized speech. As part of the voice role for the game, the advice is given through game introductions on accessibility settings and how to access them. Other settings, such as image contrast and color-blind friendly settings, are also available. An example of this is when you are scouting college players or trying to buy free agents or when you are trying to complete training.

Super Smash Bros. Ultimate

In 2018, Super Smash Bros. Ultimate, a crossover fighting game, was developed by Bandai Namco Studios and Sora Ltd. Nintendo published the game for the Nintendo Switch. It is the fifth edition of the Super Smash Bros. series.

Gameplay

Super Smash Bros. Ultimate is a fighting game – not the kind that Call of Duty is, but a fighting game nonetheless. The game is loosely based on the extremely popular Pokémon Universe of characters. The game is for up to eight players in which characters from Nintendo games and other franchises are third-party play to knock each other out of an arena. Every player has a percentage meter, which is correlated with the damage they take. The more damage a player takes, the higher that bar raises, ultimately making it easier for them to launch in the air and out of the arena. In standard battles, one of three victory conditions are used:

1. Timed – all the players aim to score the most points by defeating their opponents in a given time period.

2. Stock – the players are given a set number of lives, and to win, they have to be the last man standing.

3. Stamina – the players just have to reduce their opponents' health to zero to win the game.

Using Poké Balls and Assist Trophies, players can attack enemies or attain power-ups. In timed matches, some supporting trophies can be attacked and defeated to earn points. Each character also has a powerful final smash attack, which can be done either by getting a smash ball or filling a special meter, which can be turned both on and off. The game features 103 different stages included in the base game, packed with additional DLC fighters. They can all be played in alternate battlefield and omega variants or be toggled to overcome stage threats. A new feature called Stage Morph allows players to choose two stages that the game alternates between certain intervals during a match.

Spirits

Another set of modes revolve around a new mechanic known as spirits, replacing collectible trophies from previous games. Every single Spirit is based on a crossover character. They can be used to give a fighter unique ability that help them fight better against human or computer opponents, earning new spirits in return. Players gain spirits through pre-made challenges known as "Spirit Battles," which capture the theme of the character represented by the Spirit, one of the game's fighters and other specific level effects or is embodied by more. For example, the Spirit of Battle of Requaza of the Flying Dragon Pokémon requires players to defeat a larger version of Ridley with three new effects.

A separate spirit board mode presents a rotating set of events for players to gain Spirit. Spirits have an evolution and development system similar to the Pokémon game, leveling spirits for a powerful and more powerful effect or a means of merging new abilities into a new soul. Nintendo offers limited-time Spirit events in cross-promotion with other games and franchises, where many of them are only available to collect during the event.

World of light

Spirit Mechanic is a staple in the game's single-player adventure mode, World of Light. Mode's narrative begins with an evil entity, Galeem, who destroys the Smash Brothers' world, vaporizing almost all of the combat characters and imprisoning them; Only Kirby, due to his Warp Star, develops this attack. Players must explore the ruined world to save captured fighters and spirits by completing marked challenges. Players can use the recaptured allies and spirits to overcome some challenges on the map and eventually defeat Galeem. However, after Gleim was defeated, a new enemy, Dharkon, took power and, after being defeated, waged war against Gleim, and the players must destroy both. If only Galeem is defeated, Dhaka will engulf the world in darkness. However, if only Dharkon is defeated, Galeem will cover the universe with light. There is a route that allows players to defeat both at once. When this is done, the spirits are freed from the control of the gods and sent back to the real world.

Multiplayer

The game supports local multiplayer, local wireless with other systems, and plays through online connections. By defeating players online, players can earn tags that can be traded for in-game currency to purchase new spirits, music, and Mii fighter costumes. The game is compatible with the use of USB adapters with Joy-Con controllers, Nintendo Switch Pro controllers, and GameCube controllers. Like the previous entry, Emmy-controlled figurines can be used to create AI-controlled figure players who can be trained to become stronger. Shortly after the game's release, a service for the Nintendo Switch Online mobile app, known as "Smash World," was launched that allows players to capture images and videos from the game on social media.

In addition to sharing, it allows players to check their game statistics. The final features over 900 music tracks, which can be played via the handheld mode of the switch in standby mode. Version 3.0 of the game, released in April 2019, adds a stage builder that allows players to create their custom stages, and which they can share or download through the Switch online service. The update also includes a replay editor that allows players to edit archived replays and share them with others or download them to other devices. These will also be available within the Smash World app. An update provided limited support for Nintendo Labo's virtual reality VR kit, allowing a player to watch computer-only matches in VR or play against the computer in 1-on-1 mode.

Minecraft

Everyone knows about Minecraft – it's literally the Super Mario of this generation. Mojang Studios developed this sandbox video game. Mojang Studios created the game in the open-source Java programming language and, in 2009, released it as a public alpha for personal computers. In the game, players explore a procedurally-generated 3D world that is blocky and has infinite terrain. They may eventually discover and extract craft tools and items, raw materials and build earthworks or structures.

Gameplay

One of Minecraft's distinguishing features is that there are no specific goals to accomplish in this game. It ultimately gives players a lot of freedom to play the game on their own terms. However, there is an achievement system known as "advancement" in the Java version of the game. The gameplay is a first-person perspective by default, but players have the option of a third-person perspective. The game world is almost made up of 3D objects - mainly cubes and liquids, and commonly called "blocks" - such as furnishing various materials such as dirt, stones, ores, tree trunks, water, and lava.

The core gameplay revolves around selecting and placing these objects. While players can move freely around the world, these blocks are arranged in a 3D grid. Players can "mine" blocks and then place them elsewhere, allowing them to build things. Quite a lot of commentators describe the game's physics system as unrealistic – liquids are flowing continuously for a specific horizontal distance from the source blocks. The player can remove that by merely filtering it into a bucket or placing a solid block in its place. The game also includes a material called Redstone, which can be used to build primitive mechanical devices, electrical circuits, and logic gates for building many complex systems.

The game world originates as infinitely and procedurally as players locate it, using a map seed derived from the system clock at the time of world creation (or manually specified by the player). There are limitations on vertical movement, but Minecraft allows an infinitely large game world to be generated on the horizontal plane. Due to technical problems when arriving at extremely distant locations, there is an obstacle preventing players from tracing for locations beyond 30,000,000 blocks from the center.

The game achieves this by dividing the world's data into smaller segments called "blocks" built or loaded only when players have them. The world is divided into biomes, from deserts to forests to snowfields; The area consists of plains, mountains, forests, caves, and various lava/water bodies. The in-game time system follows a day and night cycle, and a full cycle lasts for 20 real-time minutes.

When starting a new world, players must choose one of five game modes and four difficulties ranging from peaceful to difficult. Increasing the difficulty of the game causes the player more damage from the mob, as well as other difficulty-specific effects. For example, peaceful hardship prevents hostile mobs from being born, and tough hardship allows players to starve when they die of hunger. You can easily change the difficulty once you select it. However, the game mode is locked, and only cheats can change it.

New players have the skin of randomly selected custom skins that the player can create. The players can also find various non-player characters like mobs, villagers, animals, and hostile creatures.

Farm animals, such as cows, pigs, and chickens, can be hunted for food and crafting materials. They roam during the daytime, while hostile mobs - including large spiders, skeletons, and zombies - spawn during the night or in dark places such as caves. Some hostile mobs, such as corpses, skeletons, and submerged (underwater versions of zombies), burn under the sun if they have no head.

Other creatures unique to Minecraft include Creeper (a blasting creature that snaps at the player) and Enderman (a creature with the ability to teleport as well as pick and place blocks). There are also different forms of the mob that spawn under different circumstances; For example, there are husky versions of zombies that roam the deserts.

Minecraft has two alternate dimensions in addition to the overworld (main world). The Netherlands and the End. The Netherlands is a hell-like dimension accessed through player-made portals. It has many unique resources and can be used to travel large distances in the overworld, as each block traveling in the Netherlands is equivalent to eight blocks traveling in the overworld. The player can build an alternate boss horde called Witter from materials found in the Netherlands.

The end is a wasteland containing several islands. A boss dragon called the Ander Dragon lives on the main island. Killing the Dragon opens access to an exit portal, which records the game's closing credits and a poem written by Irish novelist Julian Gough. Players are again sent back to their spawn point, and the game can continue indefinitely.

Most Popular Games
The Top Ten Esports Games by Total Prize Pool

According to the Esports Observer, the top 10 esports games by total prize pool in 2020 were the following.

1. Counter Strike $14.75 Million

2. Dota 2 $8.87 Million

3. League of Legends $8.00 Million

4. Fortnite $7.87 Million

5. Call of Duty – Modern Warfare $6.27 Million

6. Rainbow 6 $5.02 Million

7. Overwatch $4.36 Million

8. Players Unknown Battlegrounds $4.00 Million

9. Hearthstone $3.73 Million

10. Rocket League $2.63 Million

Chapter 6: Overview of Generations

*"Each generation writes its own history of generations."-**Spitzer***

The moment a child is born, a new generation separating the offspring from their parents is produced. This very concept is what elicits the ambiguity of an ever-shifting threshold in time. In our modern era, the word generation can imply a multitude of meanings. There is a natural and social element each to it. In other words, if looked at through a very simplistic lens, it applies to three things: birth, procreation, and death. However, taking a more in-depth look into it shows that it also applies to the different relationships between individuals constituted within the family and society as a whole, as that is a portrayal of the 'generation gap.'

Over the last 50 years, from the young adulthood of the Silent Generation to that of Millennials, and now on to Gen Z, there has been a significant cultural and societal shift in the United States and the world. The question now is that through all the generational differences and gaps, how is each generation different from the one that came before it? More importantly, how do they all differ from one another collectively? Before we look into that, let's look at the generally accepted breakdown of generations based on birth years.

1. Silent Generation (Traditionalists) - 1925 -1945

2. Baby Boomers - 1946-1964

3. Generation X - 1965-1976

4. Millennials (or Gen Y) - 1977-1995

5. Generation Z – 1996 - 2011

6. Gen Alpha - 2011 - 2025

The fact of the matter is that every generation has a set of similarities and differences with one another. Things that may attract younger generations are most likely not what the older ones care about. A part of it may have to do with their age differences and another part, with their generational and hence cultural differences. And what's fascinating is that these generational differences usually have no geographical boundaries. For example, those born as Gen Z ordinarily have the same characteristics in the United States as they do in other countries.

Different generations can be defined first and foremost by their interests and personality characteristics. For instance, Millennials are more likely to pay extra money for a one-time, amazing experience. In contrast, Gen Z on the other hand craves authentic *brand* experiences, something tangible and tactile. They are generally categorized as opposed to owning material goods, which makes experiential marketing supremely important to this group of consumers. When it comes to marketing brands need to realize the marketing strategies for each one of them have to be specific to their generation. So, before we dive into a discussion about marketing strategies, the first step is to understand the generations and their differences.

Silent Generation

(Born between 1925 – 1945)

The Silent Generation were the children of The Great Depression, and today they comprise roughly 20 million adults in their 70s and 80s. Their generation is awkwardly sandwiched between two better-known generations: They were born a little too late to be the heroes of World War II and a little too early to be the firebrands of a New Age. This ultimately affected their personal lives, becoming a source of tension for them. They are known as the "silent generation" because children that were born in that era were expected to be "seen and not heard."

They were born at such a time in history that automatically primed them for success. While they were just a bunch of children and teenagers when the upheavals of the Depression and World War II took place, their adulthood was during the most glorious period of sustained economic boom ever known to America. Their contributions to this burgeoning prosperity were also huge. Although it sounds like the prime reason for their success was their good timing of when they were born, there was a lot more that made them successful being fortunate enough to be born at such a prosperous time in history.

Defining the "Silents"

Their generation was a pretty traditional one. It is not surprising then that more men held a college degree in their time than women (which is the opposite of Millennials), and about 60% of women did not work outside their homes. Interestingly, of these women, 85% considered "housework" their primary occupation. That was also because a great majority of them were conservative, religious, and married. To some people from this generation, the name "The Silents" is worth objecting to. Mainly because when it came to transforming the society, they were anything but silent. Infamous people like Martin Luther King, Jr., and Gloria Steinem were a part of this generation. The leadership, speeches, and writings of these two incredible people caused vast social revolutions.

They were the generation that brought peace after their ancestors won the war. They did a great deal to bring prosperity and success. They were a generation full of passionate and driven individuals, people, who did not just talk about change, but fought for it, worked for it. While economic and geopolitical events swirled around them, they silently grew up doing their duties.

A Hardworking Generation

They carried into the factories of industrialized society the strong work ethic that they learned from their parents. Having grown up during tough times, they consider work a privilege and it shows because they are deemed as the wealthiest generation. They have a strong belief in the fact that hard work is the only way to earn your way. Since they spent long, exhausting hours in their prime, it helped them get ahead in their work and careers and they believe that everyone else should do the same. This generation does not believe in flash-in-the-pan successes. They believe that tenure and proven productivity are the only way for one to get promotions and advance in their careers. That, too, is mainly because that is how they climbed their way up the ladder. Thus, for them, it is the only way they have known and seen.

They Have Willpower

Once again, having grown up in such adverse times, misfortune does not appall them even in the slightest. They are men and women who are strong-willed, diligent, and determined. They go to the longest distances to achieve something if they want to, and hardly ever quit. I mean, it should not be a shocker because they did, after all, survive the Great Depression with their parents during their formative years. During those times, most of them had to go above and beyond to simply earn enough to survive. They did not care what the job was; they took it, worked hard for it, and were grateful to get it. Unlike the impulsive and aggressive Millennials and Gen Z's, you will never find a traditionalist storming out of an office in anger, quitting a job, and getting a different one.

Traditionalists Are Loyal Employees

These people are quite civic-minded and loyal not just to their countries but to their employers too. In their day, the bond between employer and employee was reciprocal. You were loyal to the company, and the company took care of you with benefits and pensions after you retired. Unlike the Millennials and Generation X workers, most traditionalists have worked for the same employers throughout their working lives. They are much less likely to switch jobs for the sake of career advancements compared to younger generations. And they are very civic-minded. Even today, in the U.S., they register as the largest voting population block.

They Respect Authority

Since they were raised in a condescending environment, where their opinions were not heard or mattered, they were taught to respect authority. Due to this, they grew up with very traditional values as conservatives. Unlike Generation Z or Millennials, who have time and again rose against authorities and are free-spirited individuals who fight for what they believe in, they are quite the opposite. They rarely initiate conflict.

They Are Thrifty

They are not a generation who would want to trade their cars every few years. They maintain whatever they own until the property's lifespan ends. They have a habit of reusing things that may come off as annoying to the newer generations who carelessly live. Life and material possessions were not disposable. They brag about the refrigerator that lasted them thirty years.

The Silent Generation Can Be Tech-Challenged

Being the oldest generation of our time, they find it hard to adapt to new, more efficient ways of doing things - especially when it involves technology. They are great at dealing with people individually because while they were growing up, there were not many technological advancements. Millennials and Gen Z are pretty much the opposite because they hardly ever knew a time where there were no cell phones or computers.

Baby Boomers

After World War II, the average age of marriage decreased, while the number of children skyrocketed. This made the Baby Boomer's generation considerably larger than their predecessors. This population explosion conveniently corresponded with a post-war economic boom. However, because the population only suddenly increased, in the early years of this boom, many schools were overcrowded, colleges failed to provide enough seats, and there was intense competition for starting jobs. Consequently, the young Baby Boomers had to learn to compete for success and resources. Common characteristics held by most people of this generation are as follows:

Work-Centric

Their generation is filled with remarkably hardworking people. They are motivated by prestige, perks, and position. In their professional lives, they tend to enjoy long work weeks, often defining themselves by their accomplishments. Growing up in an extremely competitive time, they had to make a lot of sacrifices to get where they are in their careers. Thus, they hold a firm belief that Millennials and Generation X should also conform to a culture of overwork and become workaholics. They often end up critiquing the younger generations for their lack of ethics and commitment to any workplace.

Independent

Baby Boomers grew up in an era of reform, and so they think that they can change the world, because they basically did. This makes them independent, self-reliant, and confident individuals. They challenged the status quo and questioned established authority. In their workplaces, unlike the prior generation, they do not hesitate to challenge established practices and are certainly not afraid of confrontation.

Goal-Oriented

Since they had better financial and educational opportunities compared to the previous generations, they are career-oriented and dedicated individuals. They like to take up challenging projects and always strive hard to make a difference. They are motivated by developments in their professional lives and love having their expertise acknowledged and valued.

Competitive

To Baby Boomers, the position they hold in their careers defines their self-worth. Thus, they can be very competitive in workplaces. They are full of resources, and their goal is to win. Their conservative beliefs in a hierarchical structure and rankism tend to give them a hard time settling in workplaces with flexibility trends. With regards to technology, if we concluded that the Silent Generation is "technology challenged," then we could label the Baby Boomers as "technology learners," or as I like to call them; digital immigrants. Everything that is new in technology has been introduced to boomers after they have adopted other life rituals and ways of living their life. Every single bit of technology, therefore, needs to be learned and adapted into their current lives. Since, as humans, we are resistant to change, the technology learning curve becomes steep for boomers who do not interact naturally with the technological world around them. Subsequent generations, therefore, are referred to as digital natives. They have never known a life without the technology of some sort being a significant part of their existence.

Self-Actualization

The Boomers basically invented the middle class. Growing up in a time of majority middle-class affluence, these people had the energy and time for self-actualization. This led to the previous generations' values of loyalty and conformity slowly falling apart. For baby boomers, work went from being a source that provided stability to a means of self-expression and actualization.

This way, they were able to moderate the traditionalist love of hierarchical management, emphasizing equal opportunity, and structural fairness. According to Abraham Maslow's theory of psychology, *the hierarchy of needs*, self-actualized people accept themselves and others as they are. As you graduate up the pyramid of needs, self-actualization leads to a life where people lack inhibition and are able to enjoy their lives in a state of joy and free from guilt and repression.

The Baby Boomers also coincided with the peak of what we call traditional Madison Avenue advertising. Highways and the high-speed freeway system were built and now connected the country, and so advertisements proclaimed the finest products from every billboard. Televisions were purchased for every living room, so TV commercials and variety hour sponsors hawked their goods continually. If you are a fan of the television series "Mad Men," this is the greatest example of the advertising world and how they positioned products to baby boomer consumers.

Gen X

Gen X was initially known as "Gen Bust" because, unlike during the Baby Boom, the birth rates were extensively lower in this generation. The idea behind that "X" was about coming between. It was supposed that this generation did not know what they wanted. But they did know what they did **NOT** want - marriage, money, or success. Those are the things that they were told to strive for. Nevertheless, that does not mean they ended up as single, broke, and unsuccessful individuals. This can easily be seen through the fact that even today, while they only account for one-fourth of the U.S. population, their purchasing power represents 31% of the total U.S. income.

Love for Work-Life Balance

This generation values time more than money. While they do strive for further development possibilities at work, they do not put their private life at stake while doing so. They are the first generation to introduce the idea of a proper work-life balance into the professional world. They saw their predecessors work extensively long hours and become workaholics while also encouraging a hard grind. Instead of adopting their mindset and blindly following their path, Gen X professionals introduced the idea of seeking a balance of work and life together.

They are more direct

This is a generation of people who are not afraid to speak their hearts out. Compared to Millennials and Gen Z'ers, they are more direct and appreciate having honest and open conversations. They do not care about sugarcoating anything; they tell things how they are - rude or not.

Embrace Feedback

Generation X professionals do not despise negative feedback at all; they appreciate it. On the other hand, Millennials tend to get a bit shocked when they are given critical feedback. Growing up, the Millennials saw a time when even the losing team got a trophy. Therefore, Millennials are looking for ways to be praised and even coddled for their achievements. Gen X appreciates constructive criticism that can potentially improve their life and work experience. They are probably the biggest buyers of self-help books.

They have a Hybrid Relationship with Technology.

People of this generation did not grow up using the internet. However, as they reached the start of their careers, many got access to it. This was ordinarily their first basic introduction to technology, and since it was a workplace requirement to know this, they had to adapt. This gave them a unique relationship with technology, as compared to preceding generations. While they are not attached to their phones all the time, they are ardent about using emails to communicate since email is still the predominant platform for work communication. While 60% of the Millennials use their phones for over an hour a day, only 40% of Gen Xers share the same screen time. Additionally, since they did not have a lot of technology when they were growing up, they developed better interpersonal skills. This has allowed them to collaborate and make stronger connections easily in the workplace.

Millennials

Often called "Generation Y," the Millennials are known as one of the most creative and adaptive generations, especially in regards to their careers. They are already responsible for $1.3 trillion dollars of annual spending in the United States, which is 20% of the nation's total GDP. Like every generation, they come with their own set of unique characteristics, things that differentiate them from their predecessors, as well as the generation that preceded them.

Value meaningful motivation

Millennials are a generation that is motivated by creative work, things that make an impact on others and within their communities, and also love sharing their gifts. In other words, they crave intrinsic motivation. Many people of this generation can be seen working selflessly towards helping other people, improving a community or a global issue or spreading inspiration. On top of that, instead of aiming for monetary gains, they are often on the lookout for ways to expand their meaningful work. Although they have a strong professional drive that helps them in career advancements, many of them tend to do so for reasons that are not just limited to a salary increment. Self-fulfillment is an enormous motivator.

Intuitive knowledge of technology

Most Millennials have seen the extensive growth of technology while growing up. This enabled them to quickly develop the ability to change and adapt according to modernized technology as soon as it comes. In fact, they are also the first generation to be entirely globalized online during their early adulthood and adolescence. They rely greatly on smartphones, laptops, and tablets.

Open and adaptive to change

Not only are these people adaptive to change, many of them even welcome it. Most of these people understand that there are constant changes in industries and methods of working. They are not afraid of it, and they acknowledge it and work towards adaptation. This ultimately allows them to advance in their careers and opens doors to quite a lot of opportunities.

Places importance on tasks rather than time

Millennials seem to be more inclined to work than to focus on time. This can range from a production standpoint to productive outcomes, as well as a prioritization of product quality, which can be delivered or related to the work. This generation places more importance on working productivity than worrying about how many hours he can spend on the job. They don't "punch the clock," they "finish the project." Often, Millennials may want to be flexible in their programs, working outside of the "traditional 9 to 5" job, and thus may spend more of their time pursuing things outside of work. Flex hours were invented for this group.

Gen Z

Finally comes Generation Z. They are a part of a generation that is technological, social, visual, and global. Amongst all the generations, they are the most educated, sophisticated, and connected generation. They are full of young-influencers and people who do not believe in traditional values. They are not afraid to think out of the box and do things that are out of the ordinary. They comprise nearly 2 billion of the world's population, and not only do they represent the future, but they are also creating it. They were born in a time of active terrorism, climate change, recession, and the global pandemic. As a consequence, they are predicted to spend their young adult years in a time of social and economic upheaval and renewal.

Financially focused

Generation Z looks at their jobs as a means to an end. They do not feel the need to love what they do, unlike their parents. The mantra, "follow your passion." falls a little flat with this group. Their outlook towards work is that it is done strictly for financial reasons and, thus, will take on a job if it pays well, even if it is not something they are passionate about. This has been called the "Gig Economy," where freelancers and Uber drivers and Instagram creators and influencers have overtaken dreams of MBA careers on Wall Street. At the same time, this does not mean that they would not prefer to do something they love, just that it is not a necessity for them.

If they had to make a choice between earning better and doing something they love, the substantial paycheck would most likely prevail. This focus on finances is due to the fact that they saw their parents lose a great amount of money and wealth in the 2008 recession. Additionally, pursuing the same college education that their parents may have comes at a great cost, huge college debt. This ingrained this idea in their minds that money can disappear in the blink of an eye; therefore their decisions should be more financially driven. Gen Z is minimalists. There is a boon in looking at alternative living spaces, such as converting storage containers into "tiny homes."

A Generation of Entrepreneurs

More often than not, we hear stories about different people who started off with a small setup in the garage and ended up accumulating limitless wealth, people like Bill Gates, and Jeff Bezos, and Steve Jobs. These stories are motivational and inspire the Gen Z'ers to be creative and believe in their potential, thus leading countless teenagers to create apps in their free time that make them overnight millionaires. Take the founder of Twitch, Emmett Shear, for an example. Do you think he had any idea his platform would explode in popularity and be bought by Amazon for $970 million dollars? He just wanted to create a platform to address something he and his buddies had a passion for.

People of this generation are not afraid to chase their ideas and make their dreams come true. They know that an entire world of knowledge is just a click or two away, so everything they do not know, they can easily learn. This makes their bold decision to become entrepreneurs seem much less risky.

They are Tech Savvy

The people of this generation were born in a time when the internet and cellphones were commonplace and ubiquitous. Therefore, they know a great deal about technology because they basically grew up using it. They are people who crave instant gratification. They know that anything they need is always readily and easily accessible. Since they are extremely social individuals online, they have friends all around the world, whether it is through social media or online gaming. And one of the cultural touchstones is online gaming.

Generation Z wants to be heard

As they have access to limitless information, they hold strong opinions about any and everything. Additionally, they want those opinions to be heard. While they may be younger than their colleagues, they expect to be heard in the workplace and given equal importance and opportunities. They believe that their ideas are as valuable as those from members of any other generation, and their lack of experience does not change that.

A Comparison of Generations

Having discussed each generation independently, let us now see how they compare to one another in a few ways.

Education

The young adults of today are much better educated than their ancestors. Statistically speaking, the share of young adults with a bachelor's degree or higher has grown a lot in the last fifty years. Among Millennials, around four out of ten[11] (39%) have a bachelor's degree or higher, compared with just 15% of the Silent Generation, roughly a quarter of Baby Boomers, and about three-in-ten Gen Xers. For young women, the gains in educational attainment have been quite steep. Among women of the Silent Generation, only 11% had obtained at least a bachelor's degree when they were young (ages 25 to 37 in 1968). Millennial women are about four times (43%) as likely as their Silent predecessors to have achieved as much education at the same age.

Millennial men are also more educated than their predecessors. While educational achievements have grown for both men and women over the past five decades, According to Pew Research Center, Millennial women hold more bachelor's degrees compared to the men, almost as though the roles of the Silent Generation and Boomers were reversed. Women of this generation were the first to outpace men when it came to education.

Employment

As young adults, boomer women entered into the workforce, in droves consequently setting a great example for Gen X and Millennial women to follow suit. At the time of the Silent Generation, in 1966, only 40% of women were employed in any capacity. For Millennial women today, 74% are employed while just a quarter are not in the labor force. Boomer women were the turning point. As early as 1985, more young Boomer women were employed (66%) than were not in the labor force (34%).

Even though they are largely known for their job-hopping behaviors, Millennial workers are as likely as Gen X workers to stick with their employers when they were the same age. Roughly seven-in-ten of Millennials ages 22 to 37 in 2018 (70%) and Gen Xers the same age in 2002 (69%) reported working for their current employer at least 13 months. The Great Recession did affect all Americans greatly, creating a rather challenging job market for Millennials who were just starting to build careers in the workforce. The unemployment rate was

---

[11]*How Millennials compare to prior generations* Retrieved from
https://www.pewsocialtrends.org/essay/millennial-life-how-young-adulthood-today-compares-with-prior-generations/

quite high for the young adults of America in the years preceding the recession. This, in turn, impacted their future wealth and earnings.

Income and wealth

It does not come as a surprise that the Millennials have more complicated financial well-being situations. Over the past 50 years, the individual earnings for young workers have mostly remained flat. However, there is a notable gap in earnings between those Millennials who got a college education and those who did not. Likewise, the income trends for young adults' households are particularly influenced by their education.

Compared to their older generations, they appear to have accumulated a little less household wealth. Millennials with a bachelor's degree or more and a full-time job had median annual earnings valued at $56,000 in 2018, roughly equal to those of college-educated Generation X workers in 2001. Nevertheless, those Millennials who did not go to college had annual earnings lower than their equivalents in previous generations. For instance, Millennial workers with some college education reported making $36,000, lower than the $38,900 early Baby Boomer workers made at the same age in 1982. The pattern is alike for those young adults who never attended college.

Millennials in 2018 had an average household income of $ 71,400, similar to that of Gen X young adults ($ 70,700) in 2001. (This is updated in 2017 dollars and is adjusted by house size. In addition, household income includes income for young adults, and income for anyone else living in the house.)

The growing gap in education is even more evident when you look at the annual household income. For Millennials in the 25- to 37-year-olds in 2018, the average median salary was $105,300 for those with a bachelor's degree or higher, nearly $56,000 more than for homes held by high school graduates without a college degree. The difference between median income and education for previous generations ranges from $ 41,200 for the Boomers late to $ 19,700 for Silent Generation when they were young.

While young adults, in general, do not have much-accumulated wealth, Millennials have far less wealth than the Boomers did in the same years. And over 36% of Millennials without a college degree report living with their parents.

This modest difference in wealth can be due to the generation of debt. Compared to previous generations, many Millennials have both government-backed and private student loans, and the amount they owe is huge. The share of adult families with any student debt has more than doubled from 1998 (when Gen Xers were aged 20 to 35) to 2016 (when Millennials were older). In addition, the average amount of debt was almost 50% greater for Millennials with special student loans ($19,000 on average) than those with Gen X debt when they were younger ($12,800 on average).

Conclusion

There have been a great many changes across the generations. What started with a generation of conservative and religious individuals (Silent Generation) ended with a generation of the most free-spirited and open-minded individuals (Generation Z). Each one of them is unique in their own ways and hold a set of beliefs and values dear to them. We see that with time, the advancements have not just been in technologies, but also in the thinking and ways of people. As they all strive for different things and have their own set of motivators, marketing to each of the generations should be tweaked to their likings. Understanding their backgrounds can, therefore, be a great help. And exploring how brands market to each group is also worth exploring.

Chapter 7: How Advertisers Communicate

When we talk about advertising, we must realize that as every generation goes through changes throughout their lives – those changes define them. Thus, naturally, the focus is on understanding how people's wants to expand and evolve. This is consolidated with the process of diversification, expansion, and growth of a country's economy. Additionally, the vertical and horizontal development of the global market must also be factored in when preparing advertising solutions.

How Advertisements Work

The truth is that as time passes and personal economic growth expands, people wants to expand as well. Development occurs in stages, the first being the basic needs of people, as suggested by Maslow's hierarchy of needs. At this stage of human development, people do not need advertisements as they are merely seeking survival. However, when survival needs are met, people start to search for other needs, a few of which could be in the sphere of culture and art. Once the stage of satiation is reached by a society, people start searching for something higher such as exotic food and drinks, fashion in clothing rather than just protection against the elements, greater luxuries, self-fulfillment, and better entertainment, among other things.

All of this is a part of human development. As time has passed, human labor's ability to produce an overabundance has increased, thus making complicated development possible and complex living desirable. Humans are equipped well to discover new things, time and time again, causing great changes and continual disruption in their lives. Taking this pattern of development into consideration, what was once merely a source for providing information for goods and services, advertising has now taken an entirely different route. It has turned into a persuasion race in the face of various brands competing over the same product or service. Further, it focuses on the creation of new markets, wants, and lifestyles. We have finally reached a point where the world is in the process of interdependence and integration.

In the world economy, the trans-nationalization or mobility of capital across national boundaries and distribution and production is fast integrating. In this situation, there is no difference in the manufactured product of different firms. It makes localization and marketing a lot more significant. There are not many differences between the services and products offered by competing firms. Still, every company strives to achieve a monopoly over the market. Therefore, the purpose of advertising is no longer to persuade or inform. It defines a race where the winner is the company that captures the consumer's mind the best to achieve brand monopoly.

The task of advertisements is to mold the consumer's attitude or behavioral pattern. This is challenging because it has moved into the area of human social relations. It has to compete with many things ranging from traditional home influences, the school, and religious institutions to create a unique type of aspiration toward a different lifestyle. Through built-in obsolescence of existing services or products, advertising creates new wants by projecting changing fashions. Moving forward, it encourages competition and emulation between individuals and even among brands.

This is how we have reached what we call "the consumer society" today. Moreover, advertising also has an influence on the media. That is not necessarily implied in a crude way of threatening to withhold advertisements or buying media personnel. The fact that periodicals, newspapers, and even electronic media depend on advertising as a major revenue source is entirely accurate. More importantly, it should be noted that both media-owners and advertisers belong to the same sociocultural and socioeconomic levels.

Powerful industries and magnates own most media avenues. Bureaucrats who have control over state-owned media also come from the same social layer. The media have also been monopolized with the emerging monopolies in other areas. The pattern for programmed telecast or broadcast was set by sponsored programs in the electronic media. While the choice still remains, it is limited to a small number of brands offering the same service or product with almost the same user satisfaction. The choice is determined not by the quality of the product, but by the success of advertising campaigns.

In the words of American economists, Baran and Sweezy, advertising, *"in its impact on the economy, is outranked only by militarism. In all other aspects of social existence, its all-pervasive influence is second to none."* (Monopoly Capital)

Today, advertising has become a powerful instrument for motivating the public's actions and opinions. That is one of the reasons why it is used for political campaigns because its impact on people is stronger than one might believe. With an easy access to modern information and communication technology, advertising comes with the dangers of misuse by every powerful instrument that humans use.

When we talk about development in this sense, it requires understanding how stages of social progress transition from one to the other. Remember, they always move from a simpler to a more complex production, economic, and political system, as well as socio-cultural relations. The process of development has three facets: social, political, and economical.

In most cases today, the transition is from a pre-industrial to an industrial economy and society. In our era, one of the most technological and scientific revolutions is specifically in the field of communication. This transition to a more powerful communication coincides with the post-industrial information-based society. So, in this transitional period, different generations of humans co-exist, ranging from people who grew up in advanced times and those who were not equipped with it until early adulthood.

The great part about having a transitional society is how it is in this constant state of formation or movement. Additionally, this transition is in motion when the communication revolution has broken barriers of space and time. Today, the taste of affluence predominating in the more established and developed societies is brought straight into our homes. Just like democracy increases the urge for more privileges and rights, an increment in literacy is stressing over the desire for more information and knowledge. An awareness of the rousing willingness to change around the world is being created. Expectations of upward cultural and social mobility keep increasing. The world is continuously changing and moving forward. It is all a part of the development process of deciding which concepts are still useful and which new concepts need to be acquired and worked for.

In a society where change is continuous in every shape and form, information and communication must play a huge role. This directly applies to advertisements because it is one of the most modern and scientific methods of dissemination of information and motivating people across the world for a particular product or cause. In a developing society, advertising is much more than a link between the producer and consumer for making a capitalist profit.

Chapter 8: Baby Boomers and How Advertisers Communicate to Them

Baby Boomers (born between 1946 and 1964)

As you already know, baby boomers are members of the large generation born between 1946 and 1964. This generation has been portrayed in many different lights. As they grew up in an era where they had increased financial, social, and educational opportunities, they are often seen as a generation of exploration, optimism, and achievement. When they are compared to prior generations, the number of young adults who relocated away from their family to pursue a career or educational interests was much higher among them.

The post-war optimism during the late 1940s and early 1950s inspired people of this generation to hold values such as a sense of stability, prosperity, and opportunity. For many Americans, this era was the dawn of accessible long-distance travel, space exploration, and prosperity. The racial tensions in the United States increased, the Vietnam War emerged, and the self-exploration and peace movement of the 1960s started. The complexity of their collective identities greatly increased.

While the Baby Boomers grew up in a time where the economic and social equalities increased, it was also an age of conflict. The country was often torn by diverse political views, war, and social injustice. They participated in a few of the greatest social changes in the USA's history, during the 1960s and 1970s, in the Civil Rights Movement and Women's Movement. Also, they experienced dramatic shifts in economic, social, and educational opportunities.

Workplaces evolved from being a fairly racially homogeneous, paternalistic environment to one with increased gender and racial diversity. The rapid social and political changes of the nation started to reflect in the workplace. Terms such as "equal opportunity workplace" and the "glass ceiling" were coined by this generation. They started to use personality profiles to become aware of how to get along with all co-workers. Baby boomers grew up in an entirely different era than today. Thus, their way of living is somewhat between the values they dearly hold and the trends of our day. They did not have smartphones or Netflix. They were kids who played physical sports with each other. They were kids who actually stepped outside their houses, instead of having their eyes glued to screens.

History of Advertising in the 1950s

American advertising history is fascinating to a great extent. If you compare times, you will be amazed to see how much time has caused changes in visual aesthetics. Due to the wars, shifts in the economy, and advancements in technology, consumer's needs were continually changing. While every decade has its own style of advertising, the 1950s really stand in contrast to what we are accustomed to today. With so much happening altogether, there were endless advertising opportunities, and people knew that.

The bottom line is that the 1950s were quite a unique time. It was considered both the Golden Age of Television and The Golden Era of 3D Cinematography. It was a time of great music where an artist like Elvis changed music and changed the world. The Boomers naturally get this infamous title due to the Baby Boom that happened after the Second World War. There was a rise in targeting specific demographics. Teenagers who were creating their own subculture for the first time in history were viewed as a lucrative demographic to target. This is because their incomes were highly disposable, and they had an influence on their parents' spending habits. In the United States, far-reaching advertising trends were established in the cultural and economic environment of the 1950s. Traditional media such as radio, newspapers, and magazines remained vital ad conduits during the early years of the decade, but television quickly became the cornerstone of many advertisers' national media plans.

Decade of consumerism

Consumerism and advertisement were catching up in the U.S. until about 1953. Products like refrigerators, automobiles, and appliances, which were once in short supply during and immediately after World War II, were again plentiful. The U.S. ramped up and showed off its industrial might and the world took notice. Steady growth in manufacturing was fueled by pent-up demand for consumer products. However, a period of acute consumption followed in the latter part of the decade. "New and improved" products were being offered by marketers to keep up with high consumer demand. Newly popular methods, such as demographic targeting, generational marketing, and motivational research, were a few focused selling techniques that were relied upon during that time.

The baby boom, in turn, caused a housing boom. They all needed places to live! And thanks to the creation of the modern highway system, the suburbs were born. By the time the decade was over, one-third of the U.S. population was living in suburban areas that surrounded traditional large metropolitan centers or cities, enticed by the progress in transportation options and affordable housing for America's new middle class. This led to an undying need for new appliances and other necessities to fill those new homes. Therefore, marketers started introducing new kinds of products, while the manufacturers stirred out new automobiles, consumer electronics, and appliances. For increased productivity and leisure time, many advertised products that promoted labor-saving automation. The technical innovations of wartime were claimed by capitalism and transformed into labor-saving convenience products. "Keeping up with the Jones's" was leveraged by advertisers by instilling the fear of missing out in this newly consumerized generation.

Advertising family values

During this period of time, advertising reflected a deliberate return to traditional family values. The still lingering memories of the Great Depression were now being replaced by more positive images and futuristic portrayals of the idealized modern family. Common depictions included all the members of a family enjoying the comforts of their new home, the leisure time they got to spend together, and the extreme convenience automobiles brought into their lives. For the first time in the history of advertisements, children were targeted. Radios, magazines, records, phonographs, soft drinks, and even clothing, among other products, found a responsive teen audience.

The society's upward prosperity and mobility were also portrayed through advertisements. It showed that instead of sulking in the after-effects of the Great Depression and World War II, people were finally getting their lives back together. There was a newfound optimism within them and it showed. For instance, time and time again throughout the 1950s, advertisements promoted how necessary it was to be a two-car family. A decade that began with 59% of American families owning a car ended with most, if not all, owning at least one car while many were owning several.

By the mid-1950s, packaged goods and cigarettes were surpassed by automobiles, as the most heavily advertised products. In the mid-1950s, car owners saw their vehicles as an extension of themselves. The fast-paced changes in design pushed the consumers to replace their cars yearly, for style, not convenience. With its distinctive fins and heavy emphasis on chrome, the nation's infatuation with new technology, the atomic age, and jet planes, was reflected through advertisements.

T.V.'s coming of age

The most important factor that influenced advertising in the 1950s was the maturation of television into a viable medium. Regular live network service reached the West Coast through microwave transmitters, establishing coast-to-coast national coverage by 1951. Early T.V. programming was advertiser-sponsored, just like the radio. Advertising agencies started to produce television shows alongside networks that offered little more than their facilities, airtime, and occasional guidance. The name of the sponsor was typically promoted instead of the star.

Huge U.S. agencies like McCann-Erickson or Barton Durstine greatly benefited from representing durable and packaged goods advertisers that were quite well-known, such as Bristol-Myers, Westinghouse Electric, and Colgate-Palmolive. The television spending was $12.3 million in 1949, but it had grown to $128 million within two years. By the time it was 1954, the lead medium for advertising was T.V. Many stars, and their audiences moved from network radio to television, causing the former great losses. Around a decade later, by 1960, 90% of household penetration was covered by homes that owned televisions.

Quite a lot of agencies started to use motivational research to aid advertisers in influencing their consumers. This was done based on their need for safety, sex, belonging, and success. Consumers' spending habits were examined through psychological tools. Personalities like The Marlboro Man, Maidenform Woman, and The Hathaway Shirt Man were created, so the everyday consumer would relate to or aspire to become them. Consequently, the personification of products became a prominent tactic. In any age, advertising is shaped by a lot of factors; the social, political, and cultural environments of the time play a vital role.

Communicating to Baby Boomers Today

Contrary to popular belief, advertisements today on Fox News or sending direct mail pieces no longer make the cut when marketing to Baby Boomers. When it comes to generational marketing, one needs to understand that it is not about stereotyping an entire generation but about observing prevalent behaviors among similarly aged people. That is what digital marketing strategies should consider. Baby Boomers are an active audience who are highly engaged and also spend a good chunk of their time online. As an example, kids today fled from Facebook for other social platforms because they didn't want to be seen in the same place as Mom or Grandma.

For some time now, the marketing world has been obsessed with appealing to Millennials. In the chase to achieve that, they often overlook the fact that it is the baby boomers who control over 70% of the nation's disposable income. One of the reasons for that is that they wrongfully assume that Baby Boomers lack digital affinity. Since most of them are now entering their retirement lives, this is a great opportunity for marketers to reach out to them. As they make up such a huge segment of the consumer population, one must know how to speak to their needs and wants. Below are a few tips advertisers should keep in mind while marketing to boomers.

They are Specific

A good part of the boomer's lives is already over. On the back nine as you might say. Most, if not all, have retired and are ready to sit back and enjoy their hard-earned money. In fact, baby boomers are expected to transfer $30 trillion in wealth to younger generations over the next decade or so. The total amount expands to $68 trillion if you include the youngest boomers and look out over the next twenty-five years. This jaw-dropping amount has led to this being referenced as the "great wealth transfer." The impact on subsequent generations will be astounding. It is estimated that by the year 2030, millennials will be five times richer than they are today.

This would be the largest wealth transfer in modern history. This wealth transfer will be a tremendous shot in the arm for the Millennial generation as they have simply struggled to reproduce their parent's wealth due to difficult environmental factors, such as slower wage growth, higher cost of living and a more sluggish world economy. Boomers therefore have a positive reaction to information that proves how a product is worth their money. When advertisers are crafting their marketing message, they ensure that they highlight precisely how it will be beneficial to boomers. They tend to explicitly explain what they are offering impacts their lives positively in various aspects.

They do so by showcasing clear benefits by using specific headings and bullet points to convey their key selling points. When they format their content like this, it makes it easier to understand and helps the consumer digest information faster. When they are writing for boomers, they make sure that they also focus on how that product is worth their overall financial investment. That is because while boomers have a great buying power, they appreciate understanding all the benefits of the product that they are buying. They want to be smart buyers.

Create compelling videos

Baby boomers generally prefer information told through slow video formats, explaining concepts in grand detail. This type of media format helps them understand the information and messages that a brand presents. In media terms these videos are ordinarily called "explainer" videos. Brands tend to try different video formats, such as slideshows or animations until they find what works best for their target audience. Moreover, while boomers do not mind watching longer video content, good videos are often kept short and to the point. That helps brands focus on one concept at a time, hence assisting the audience in quickly digesting information.

Do NOT call them old

One of the biggest pet peeves of the baby boomer generation is someone referring to them as "old" or "elderly." It is a pretty straightforward rule – these words are often viewed as derogatory in the American culture, but especially to the boomer who considers themselves nowhere near "old". Quite a lot of baby boomers are still going out and living their lives to the fullest even though they are in their mid-sixties. These people do not view their age as a constraint on their ability to pursue anything that makes them happy. Modern medicine has also extended the average lifespan significantly over the past fifty years as well, so not only are people generally living longer, they are living healthier, active lives.

Marketers use this to their advantage by empowering these users to achieve all their goals. They ensure that they treat these customers as though they are a little younger than they actually are, offer them respect, show enthusiasm, and emphasize clear communication. This practice helps brands resonate with the baby boomer target market.

Slang is off the table

A general rule that advertisers follow while marketing to baby boomers is avoiding slang. When generation-specific language is used, older users feel alienated, and the business often appears insincere and insensitive. This concept especially applies to baby boomers. When slang is used, miscommunication can easily occur because of their lack of understanding or clarity. This is why when brands reach out to baby boomers, they ensure that they create concise and clear advertising content.

Use Facebook

Far more than any other social media platform, baby boomers use Facebook. They use it to stay in touch with their family and friends and stay informed with the latest news. Therefore, when marketers want to target this specific demographic, they do so over Facebook.

Facebook obviously needs no introduction, however as a brief bit of background, the world's most-famous and largest social network was launched by Mark Zuckerberg while he was a student at Harvard University, in early 2004. "The Facebook," as it was originally known, was intended to serve an online version of the 'face books' held by Harvard's various colleges – paper directories containing images and personal information about students. At first it was initially limited to students of Harvard University, and then quickly expanded to include students at other elite universities. Eventually all university and high school students in the US and Canada were able to join. In 2006, the strategic decision was made to open the site up to the general public and the rest, as they say, is history.

As an example, Facebook posted $21.2 billion in advertising revenue in Q3 2020, comprising 99% of the company's total revenue. Ad revenue grew by 22.1% in Q3 compared to the same three-month period a year ago. (Facebook Inc. "Form 10-Q for the quarterly period ended September 30, 2020)

As a comparison, according to industry data, local radio digital advertising revenue in the United States surpassed one billion U.S. dollars in 2019. At that time, it was projected that the figure would further grow to $1.29 billion by the end of 2020. That's for the ENTIRE year. And baby boomers were right there at the top of the demographics for Facebook usage.

To conclude, the bottom line is that baby boomers are loaded with money that they want to spend. Therefore, advertisers must ensure that they communicate with them in ways that are specific to their demographic. Every generation needs to be targeted according to their cultural values and social practices – that is what attracts them the most.

Chapter 9: Gen X and How Advertisers Communicate To Them

Gen X - (born between 1965 - 1980)

Marketing strategies, like technology evolve over time. If you look at the historical progression of advertising, you will notice patterns in marketing strategies and the masses' mindsets. Each generation looks for something different in the products they want to buy. For instance, if the late boomers were looking for a house, they would seek out marketing messages targeting mortgages, house size, and locality. Simultaneously, if Millennials were looking for a house, they would be interested in the most modern features such as granite countertops, stainless steel appliances, smart lighting and energy saving. It's a simple example, but it highlights how marketing strategies have evolved over time.

Advertisements in the 80s

As cable channels prospered, they undermined the influence of traditional broadcast networks. Cable TV had a profound effect on restructuring the media industry during the 1980's. By the early 1990s, the once-dominant broadcast networks saw their share of the evening TV audience slip to less than 60%. The three major powerhouse networks, ABC, NBC, and CBS each claimed about 19% of the TV audience, while "independent" TV and cable TV, as exemplified by CNN (launched in 1980) and MTV (1982), captured more than 40%.

In addition to cable TV, the introduction of the recordable VCR allowed viewers to manage, organize, and control the available programs. Also, remote controls gave TV viewers the ability to "zip" and "zap" their way through TV commercials. The term "zipping" was coined to describe the practice of using a remote control to change channels during the commercials. Viewers could also "zap" commercials out of recorded programs by fast-forwarding through them, thus ignoring the advertised messages. Eventually, certain VCRs were marketed that could be programmed to automatically skip commercials, compounding the problem further for advertisers. (The equivalent today in digital advertising are ad blocking software and cord cutting. According to Forbes, 47% of today's online users utilized software that blocks advertisements. Additionally, Millennials and now even more so Gen Z are notorious for cutting the cord entirely and not paying for cable television subscriptions, opting instead to consume their content online or in bursts, called binge watching from services like Netflix, Hulu, or Roku).

Cable TV also contributed to the internationalization of advertising. CNN became a global network, and therefore, sold advertising globally, creating opportunities for companies for marketing their products to a worldwide audience. An innovative form of electronic advertising, direct-response home shopping services, developed in the 1980's. Home Shopping Network (launched in 1982) and QVC home-shopping networks paid cable operators a percentage of the profits from sales generated in their viewing area instead of buying airtime from cable operators.

The promotional pitches marketed as infomercials became one of the fastest-growing areas in TV advertising. These 30-minute commercials often featured celebrities and appeared as news or informational programming. In one of the biggest success stories to date, there have been over 100 million George Foreman grills sold, probably the most lucrative sports marketing deal of all time.

To maximize profits and enhance ad effectiveness, agencies made a change in the mid-1980's to 15-second TV spots, moving away from the traditional 30-second standard. This drastic change of life for ads was quite beneficial for advertisers. It doubled the number of ads run and reduced the cost per ad. It resulted in maintaining and often increasing revenue levels. The change of this magnitude posed a new creative challenge to the industry, which had to pack the motivation to purchase as well as product information into a shorter micro-sized message. They also drew critics who claimed they were cluttering the airwaves.

Advertisements in the 90s

In the 1990s, advertising faced new economic and social changes. The birth rate in the United States declined as the baby boom generation aged. Consequently, family units became smaller. Similarly, both minority and immigrant groups started to grow. The population shifted toward the sunbelt states, and there was an emergence of new markets. The mass media audience expanded through advancements in technology. New technologies, such as the internet, fragmented the audience. The mass media environment grew increasingly sophisticated and expensive, as consumers were provided with more control choices and a greater capacity for interacting with sources of advertising information.

New challenges

Specialized consultants started to insert themselves into the traditional relationships of clients and agencies. In interactive media, database marketing, and other market segments', areas that were defined by race, ethnicity, and values, experts appeared. Marketers who were unhappy with the services of the large agency holding companies with their legacy knowledge, but who didn't have a sophisticated level of knowledge and expertise in these new platforms, now had suitable assistance working as independent contractors. Many agencies moved to expand their capabilities as they awoke to this challenge. Advertising finally stepped into a period of transition: the functions, structure, and size of agencies began to change, alongside the nature of advertiser-agency relationships.

Some advertisers sought the services of multiple agencies based on platform or target audience, while others moved to consolidate accounts at fewer ones. Even others brought their accounts in-house and hired their own group of digital marketing experts. Advertisers started to cut back on their ad spending, as the need to reach a global audience in an ever-expensive mass media environment increased. Agencies and advertisers were both on the lookout for the most effective media outlets to reach the largest audience at the lowest price.

While some advertisers maintained traditional organizations, others such as General Motors Corp., Ameritech Corp., and General Mills made drastic decisions. They allowed their internal managers and marketers to control advertising decisions and perform faster promotional activities. Additionally, advertisers have begun to divert their money from advertising to promoting products and services, thereby increasing the sponsorship marketplace.

Small, creative boutiques were set up as established agencies lost their creative talent., Their highly productive workforce left to start their own companies. Small regional shops sprang up as new technologies made the agency's virtual space more valuable. Advertisers and organizations relied on modern means of communication to find and provide services from far and wide, disrupting an industry that had more or less worked the same way for over fifty years.

Established agencies have responded, creating niche units to help specific clients. Specialized private organizations focused on specific groups of people, and with technology becoming an increasingly important tool in marketing, many organizations added separate digital-focused departments.

A New Frontier: The Internet

The vision of commerce that the internet promised by beginning in the mid-1990s offered consumers many benefits. These included the ability to purchase the precise services and goods they needed at competitive prices, fast-paced, and from the comfort of their homes. The launch of many Internet-based companies, such as eBay or Amazon, was also fueled by the former promise. Initially, a single product or service was offered by many internet companies. The most obvious example is that in 1995, Jeff Bezos started Amazon as an online bookstore only, working out of his garage with just a handful of employees. We all know how Amazon has since disrupted multiple industries by scaling and expanding into almost every product, service, or even food that people purchase and consume.

The face of advertising in every shape or form was changed through technology. Since computers were now being used to create and alter images, it meant that spots could be made quite simple or really complex. This also led to emphasizing on outdoor and nature imagery. It can be observed in examples where polar bears drink Coke, handled by Creative Artists Agency as part of its "Always" campaign for Coca-Cola, or Jeep's burrowing beneath snowdrifts in an award-winning TV spot from agency Bozell titled "Snow Covered" for the automaker in 1994.

Characteristics of Generation X workers

Gen X workers have some very specific characteristics. Knowing them makes it easier to market products and services to them. Therefore, to understand how they are targeted for marketing, we must first see what kind of values and attributes they hold.

Values

- Contribution
- Feedback and recognition
- Autonomy
- Time with manager or supervisor at work

Attributes

- Adaptability
- Independence

Work-style

- High-quality end results
- Productivity
- A balance between work and life – work to live, not live to work
- Flexible work hours/job sharing appealing
- Free agents
- See self as a marketable commodity and work to create their own "brand"
- Comfortable with authority but not impressed with titles
- Technically advanced
- Ethnic diversity

Ethnic and cultural issues/implications

Advancements in technology and exposure to music television brought different cultures into the living rooms of this generation. MTV had only played white artists until the first music video by a black artist, Michael Jackson's Billie Jean, was played. Single-parent and blended families helped this generation understand that families come in all shapes and sizes. They have grown more inclusive of others and accepted differences better than the previous generation. Gen X embraced diversity in social settings. Television also helped to knock down class barriers that traditionally stereotyped racial minorities. TV shows in the 1970's such as Good Times, Sanford and Son, and Chico and the Man, portrayed minority life as living a poor life in the ghetto. Breakthrough shows in the 1990's such as The Cosby Show and the Fresh Prince of Bel Air, collapsed a lot of those stereotypes.

Generational perspectives of work / life balance

For this generation, career growth has evolved toward work and life services. Companies adopted flexible work arrangements and work/life services to meet their needs. Generation X employees have responded overwhelmingly to flexible work arrangements when available. Primary reasons for adopting flexible work arrangements and other work/life programs for Generation X are child care, two-parent working families, continuing education, personal health, personal interest unrelated to the family, and adult care responsibilities. Fast forward to the pandemic of 2020, and these remote, virtual work arrangements exploded in popularity as companies had no choice but to let employees work from home. Gen X led the way in embracing these disruptions to their usual work arrangements.

Common Gen X issues

This generation has been much better than previous generations in saving money. Gen Xers have taken advantage of 401(k) accounts, beginning this investment much earlier in their work-life, and they have not waited to put money aside for their children. For those parents determined to raise their children with less dependence on daycare, many seek part-time employment, depend on extended family-assisted daycare, or stay at home, creating some drain on family finances. Although quite good at managing money, savings are inevitably affected when having only one partner working full time.

Legal issues

- Divorce
- Child custody and support

Although the divorce rate for this generation is generally lower than national averages, overall, the divorce rate is still extremely high and will continue to be a social and legal factor. Unfortunately, as Generations X's parents divorced at an astounding rate, divorce is viewed to be quite normal by this generation. Consequently, divorce and child custody will continue to remain legal issues for this generation.

Marital/family issues

- Career vs. marriage and family
- Parenting roles
- Relationships

When Generation X entered the job market, many stressors on the economy limited job availability, affecting their ability to obtain meaningful work. Many of this generation were forced to return home at an age when independence would typically be the norm. Factors such as financial dependence on parents and generational expectations for women to work and contribute significantly to household income have narrowed the choices for this generation when choosing to marry or begin a family. As career opportunities increased and this generation began to enter into meaningful work, as many as 43% were earning minimum wage and struggling to survive. For this generation, the age of marriage increased to an all-time high, as people waited until their late 20s and early 30s to tie the knot.

Medical issues

- Pregnancy

- Smoking-related health issues

Although Gen X took their time to develop careers, delayed marriage and postponed having children, they came around to buying homes and having children at a higher rate than ever. In 1998, the birth rate had increased 2 percent, the first increase in birth rates in seven years. By the year 2000, close to two-thirds, or 65 percent, of women aged 25 to 34 had children.

Smoking-related health issues also begin to climb, as smoking rates for ages 25 to 44 years have the highest prevalence at 25.6 percent, as was reported by the Centers for Disease Control and Prevention in 2003. The smoking rate for men in this age group is 28.4 percent, while for women, it's 22.8 percent.

Mental health issues

- Depression

- Anxiety

- Eating disorders

Depression and anxiety are common issues among this generation due to the many stressors related to upbringing and social expectations. Divorce rates, which climbed quickly during their developmental years and into young adulthood, have contributed to the incidence of depression among them. Yet, delayed treatment for mental illnesses such as depression is not uncommon because divorce is often viewed as normal. Also, the fear of being perceived as weak and less competitive in the marketplace forces Gen X to seek help. Confusion and anxiety related to developing meaningful intimacy are also significant issues for this generation.

Over 72 Percent of Generation X Uses the Internet to Research Businesses

Despite their preference for traditional TV and newspapers, Generation X'ers tend to research businesses on the internet. So, even if you are running TV commercials, radio ads, or even newspaper ads, you would want to make sure your online presence is spotless.

If you have a great TV commercial, but your business looks bad online, slow loading and non-responsive website, incorrect information, or bad reviews, Generation X consumers will see that and turn to a competitor.

Marketers made sure to make their businesses look good across the most popular websites and directories.

Below are a few tactics used to address Generation X:

- Listing on Google or Bing
- Website
- Yelp
- Popular online directories

Generation X is active on Social Media too.

- 95 percent use Facebook
- 35 percent use LinkedIn
- 25 percent post regularly on Twitter

Since such a high percentage of Generation X'ers use Facebook, this social media platform is primarily used to market to them. Marketers made sure to tailor their posts to them and did not forget to target this age group when creating Facebook ads.

How Marketers enhanced their business content to approach their targeted audience (Gen-X)

- Added a description in Facebook Page's About section

- Made sure their address, website, phone number, and hours are correct

- Added a call-to-action to their Facebook Page (see "Watch Video" in the above screenshot)

- Added locations

- Managed their Facebook Reviews

- Posted regularly (at least weekly)

- Got more followers and improved engagement to show that their business is worth the follow or the purchase

- Tried Facebook advertising

Generation X Has the Highest Brand Loyalty across All Generations

Companies had previously reported that Gen Xers are loyal to the products they love. As long as you can get them in the door and give them a good experience, they remain loyal.

Returning customers are responsible for generating 40 percent of the store's revenue, so retailers are careful to do what they can to keep Generation X customers loyal.

Gen X Fidelity: Advertisers are careful to return this loyalty in some way, whether it's a discount after a certain number of purchases or a simple thank you email.

Advertisers make sure that they provide excellent service. It may seem like a no-brainer, but they knew about treating this person with respect and giving them a great experience. This allows businesses to enjoy more spending from Gen X consistently.

Returning customers spend more on average purchases, and 68 percent of people are willing to spend more money on businesses with good service.

Buyers of Generation X are Nostalgic

Google did a YouTube survey to find out what Generation X looks like most. As it turns out, the most common theme was nostalgia. Gen Xers wants to watch videos related to the past:

- Past events
- The old people
- Classic TV commercials
- Classical music

Nostalgia Marketing: Advertisers have added a little nostalgia to their marketing. Creating content in the style of their favorite TV shows or commercials of the past, has given them an intrigue within Generation X's customers.

54% of Generation X Consumers Feel Overlooked by Brands and Marketers

Everyone wants to know how to market to Millennials or Generation Z, but that can mean that we ignore Generation X.

Maybe it's because they're a smaller generation, or perhaps it has something to do with the fact that the younger generations appear to be more tech-savvy.

No matter the reason, marketers can't afford to ignore Generation X. They have a ton of purchasing power, and they are brand loyalists.

Gen X marketing: Marketers make sure that when marketing to Generation X, they create messages tailored to their goals, likes, and place in life.

Marketers let them know they are specifically talking to them. They also use nostalgia to bring them back to a simpler time or at least make them laugh and forget that they are advertising to Gen X.

This was one of the most crucial tactics used by marketers on Generation X consumers. It gained them loyal customers who return to their business time and time again.

Keeping the Humanity in Tech

Just as Gen X shouldn't be counted out as a consumer, their perspective as marketers should be considered as well. Gen X played a crucial role in developing emerging technologies, while they're also the only working generation to remember the marketing world before the digital revolution.

As the makers and marketers of these innovations, Gen X can bridge the gap between the digital and physical worlds to ensure we use technology responsibly.

By 2020, 50% of all online searches will be conducted by voice. As this shift happens, we must remain conscious of not losing our humanity – even if it means remaining polite and using manners when conversing with the AI. As early adopters and innovators of tech, Gen-X marketers can help strike a proper balance as tech natives come of age, and we drift closer to an on-demand society, needing a human touch and seamlessly fitting into peoples' lives.

The Legacy of Gen X

As digital marketing enters its next iteration and consumer preferences continue to evolve, there's already a lot of discussion around how Millennials and Gen Z will be serviced. Gen Xers are poised to answer the call.

While it's tempting to predict future trends and engagement strategies, it's in the marketers' best interest to fully understand and appreciate the influential demographics that are already of age.

Although they're often in the shadows of their parents' and children's generations, Gen X has emerged as a powerful segment for brands to target. From their evolving interests and increasing agelessness among consumers to the importance of human-centric engagements in a tech-driven world, Gen Xers are a salient test case for the future of marketing. Consequently, they are an invaluable segment for modern advertisers.

Chapter 10: Millennials and How Advertisers Communicate To Them

Millennials are a much misunderstood generation. Their behavior has been massively shaped by two significant factors. Explosive growth in student debt and the Great Recession, which hit them harder than older generations. Before we talk about how advertisers communicate to Millennials, we must understand how it was like growing up as a Millennial. For that, we will take a trip down the memory lane and go back to a time when Millennials were much younger.

History of the Millennials
(Born between 1981 – 1996)

Millennials (also known as Generation Y) are the demographic following Generation X, and preceding Generation Z. Researchers use the early 1980's as starting birth years, with 1981 to 1996 a widely accepted defining range for the generation. The Millennials are made up of individuals who reached young adulthood in the early 21st century. The Millennials grew up as gamers. They witnessed an exponential rise in the popularity of video games. This, in turn, rewired how this generation approaches teams, work, and communication. When you play a game, it offers constant feedback loops, opportunities to make a difference by saving the world, and global collaboration.

Marketing strategies have evolved with time, just like technology. But the one thing that remains consistent is that advertisers look to meet the consumer where they are spending the most time. Traditionally that has been television, live sporting events, concerts, and other types of viewable recreational activities. But millennials were the generation that started to include video gaming into that mix, and it lit the spark that started the revolution.

According to Ari Fox, CEO of Gamecon and founder of the CEC (Casino Esports Conference), "Video gaming and now esports are a cultural phenomenon and not just a new sport. It is part of the entertainment package that is now included into the fabric of our American youth."

Just as is social media, influencers, streaming personalities, and other varying modes of entertainment, in the past we had television and movies. The phone was only used to talk on, and it connected to the wall with a cord. (Think about that for a moment Gen Z)

As Ari states, "Today we have so many areas and ways to access entertainment. Younger audiences, the conventional athletes and their fans, see video gaming as part of their everyday mode of relaxation and socialization. The same way older people see turning on the television and relaxing on a daily basis, so do younger people turn on their gaming console to connect with their friends and be entertained." Millennials were the first generation to integrate technology into their social ecosystem, and not just use it as productivity tools.

Once these Millennials put on a headset, they start playing with their friends who may live halfway across the world. They have now put the same expectations into their workplace.

- **Millennial Mindset:** Millennials crave feedback, leaving a mark, and diverse collaboration thanks to gaming.

- **Innovation Influencer**: Nintendo.

- **Company Example:** The national chain of casual dining restaurants called Applebee's created a game. The game was called Bee Block, and they used it to have employees collaborate and compete on metrics like selling special menu items, clocking in on time, and completing quizzes about company rules. There was a 20% reduction in staff turnover and larger average tickets due to this game. This is called "Gamification" and is now often used successfully for corporate training and other productive uses.

The Year 2000

As the year 2000 approached, the biggest threat and fear was the Y2K glitch. This was the premise that all the computers in the world would just stop working because they weren't originally programmed to roll over from the last day of 1999 to the year 2000. If there were no computers, the world would grind to a halt. Hundreds of millions of dollars were spent to address this issue. On January

1, 2000, all the computers kept working as normal. A lot of fuss over nothing, other than the millions of brand new computers that were sold and the panic that it induced in a population picturing a world without technology.

The Millennials ended up becoming the first generation in history whose essential mediators of social life and information acquisition were digital technology platforms. They never really had to "adapt" to technology because they grew up surrounded by it. Thus, they have a natural knack for technological adaptability. They were the first true digital natives.

The Millennial's friendships, their perspective of the world, the structure of social networks, the way they learn and interact with brands and institutions, and their allocation of time, have all been shaped by digital technology.

- **Millennial Mindset:** Due to technology, Millennials approach learning, working, socializing, buying, communicating, and playing differently.

- **Company Example:** Airbnb, a marketplace and online hospitality provider, has a "chief executive" whose job is to rethink how employees learn, work, compete, interact, and play. Other companies like Cisco and Pandora have similar operational philosophies.

2004

By this time, Millennials had access to Google while they were in high school. It was a time when they used the internet to do the legwork for major projects. All the information about the world was at their fingertips, thanks to Google. People stopped going to libraries and started using online resources for learning complicated topics. (Millennials look at you with a glazed-over stare if you mention you did your research papers by going to the library and looking at something called microfiche.) A social network called MySpace was also on the rise by this time.

- **Millennial Mindset:** They are the first generation that considers the internet as a higher authority than their parents or teachers. They treat it as an external brain and have an entirely unique way of approaching problems.

- **Innovation Influencer:** Google

- **Company Example:** The former CEO of Burberry, Angela Ahrendts, created a "Strategic Innovation Council" as she saw an opportunity to leverage the different thinking and resourcefulness of Millennials. Here, they would monthly come together with leads of companies who had one single goal - innovate Burberry's future.

2005

By this time, most Millennials found their way onto Facebook. They quickly amassed hundreds of friends, leveraging social media to collaborate, contribute, and consume.

- **Millennial Mindset:** Millennials were early adopters (ex: social media, cell phones, and texting) and sought out chances to innovate, particularly as they entered the workforce.

- **Innovation Influencer:** Facebook.

2007

By the time this group was turning 17, Apple had launched the iPhone. The primary reason behind the iPhone's success was successful was that it specifically catered to Millennials. It had a multi-touch interface, virtual keyboard, automatic spell check and correction, predictive text technology, and the ability to learn new words. Due to its launch, 2007 became the first year when the number of text messages by the Americans was higher than their monthly number of phone calls. The previous AOL instant messaging days were now transferred onto iPhones, making texting a new yet common communication medium among the trendy youth.

As a side note, I had the privilege of working on the executive team at Apple for over ten years, helping to run the education sales and marketing group. Being at Apple as they introduced disruptive, life-changing technologies one after another, the iPad, iTunes, and then the iPhone, was truly one of the great thrills and honors of my entire life. I saw firsthand as I worked with schools and colleges across the country how these technologies in the hands of this Millennial generation was like handing them magic. Millennials held more computing power in their hand than sent the first men to the moon in 1969.

- **Millennial Mindset:** Technology has shaped the communication of Millennials (and every other generation).

- **Innovation Influencer:** iPhone and texting.

2008

By 2008, Twitter and Tumblr became common and extremely popular. Millennials learned the art and power of blogging, so many of them started their own personal blogs. They shared their passions on public and global platforms. They created their own personal brand. Growing up with such easy access to the internet really encouraged Millennials to have a voice and contribute to society. Brands needed to adjust quickly and realize that advertising was no longer just one-way communication.

- **Millennial Mindset:** Millennials are looking for an active role and immediate impact because they are contributors (not passive consumers or employees).

- **Innovation Influencer:** Twitter and blogging.

2011

Millennials hold relationships and lifestyles to a higher value over work. They do not mind choosing a city before they secure a job. At this point, many Millennials were in college or graduated, looking for jobs. Cities like Seattle and Austin and San Francisco and Atlanta became hot, hip popular choices due to technological friendly cultures and socially progressive ideals.

- **Millennial Mindset:** Since they always turned to their social networks to stay in touch, connect with a brand, find new opportunities, and acquire news, they are heavily influenced by their peers.

- **Innovation Influencer:** LinkedIn and crowdsourcing.

The technological advances only kept going uphill from here, and Millennials kept adjusting to these changes. The fact of the matter is that their predecessors grew up in an entirely different world. They did not have access to technology until they were at least adults. They did not grow up playing video games or chatting with strangers on the internet. Their culture and values significantly differ from that of the Millennial generation. Therefore, marketers must ensure multiple things to target them when advertising. Before exploring how marketers appeal to Millennials, let me first enlist a few differences they have with the previous generations, as backed up by research.

Generation Differences - Millennials versus Prior Generations

Millennials are a widely studied generation, and many surveys suggest numerous ways in which they are different from older generations. For instance, a survey[12] revealed that unlike Boomers and Gen Xers, Millennials are likely to describe themselves as politically independent. Additionally, a different survey[13] found that they wanted businesses to focus more on "purpose and people." It is no surprise then that countless studies on Millennials, especially those conducted on the patterns they have at work, are driven by concerns that Millennials are following radically different career trajectories compared to the previous generations. Cause marketing became a big thing.

Education

Millennials are more highly educated and aware when compared to older generations. The rate of college enrollment among them is higher. Consequently, the completion rates have also been increasing, *"with 39.4 percent of those starting at a four-year institution in 2007 graduating in four years and 59.4 percent graduating within six years[14]."* Interestingly, although a higher number of Millennials have been going to college, they do not show an increased inclination

---

[12]*Pew Research Center, "Millennials in adulthood: Detached from institutions, networked with friends,"* March 7, 2014, Retrieved from http://www.pewsocialtrends.org/2014/03/07/Millennials-in-adulthood/.
[13]*Deloitte, "Mind the gaps: The 2015 Deloitte Millennial Survey," 2015,* Retrieved from http://www2.deloitte.com/global/en/pages/about-deloitte/articles/Millennialsurvey.html.
[14]*Department of Education, National Center for Education Statistics, Digest of Education Statistics, 2014, table 326.10,* Retrieved from https://nces.ed.gov/programs/digest/d14/tables/dt14 326.10.asp.

to do majors in subjects like science, technology, mathematics, and engineering. In all STEM majors except for computer and information sciences, Millennials proportionately trail Boomers. They are choosing to major in social science and history (10.5%), business (21.7%), health professions (7.5%), and visual and performing arts (5.6%)[15].

Excessive Student Debt

With a high college attendance among Millennials comes the explosion in student debt. During the 1995–96 school year, the approximate midpoint of when the Gen Xers were in college, 25.6 percent of all undergraduates at two- and four-year colleges had student loans[16].

In the 2008-09 school year, the percentage rose to 46.6%, followed by the 2012-13 year when the proportion expanded to 49.4%[17].

Location choices Driven by Economic Realities

Relocation is a wish that many Millennials possess. Traditionally, post-graduation has been a typical time for Americans to move. For Millennials, some cities seem to be "magnets," as they offer the right combination of the labor market, housing, transportation, cultural, and educational opportunities. According to an analysis by the Brookings Institution, Washington, DC, continues to lead the nation in attracting Millennial in-migration, followed by Denver, Portland, and Houston[18]. However, Millennials, who make up the majority of internal migrants in the US[19] have not had such unlimited horizons due to the

---

[15]*Department of Education, National Center for Education Statistics, Digest of Education Statistics, 2014, table 322.10*, Retrieved from
https://nces.ed.gov/programs/digest/d14/tables/dt14_322.10.asp.
[16]*Department of Education, National Center for Education Statistics, Digest of Education Statistics, 1997, table 315*, Retrieved from http://nces.ed.gov/programs/digest/d97/d97t315.asp
[17]*Department of Education, National Center for Education Statistics, Digest of Education Statistics, 2014, table 331.20*, Retrieved from
http://nces.ed.gov/programs/digest/d14/tables/dt14_331.20.asp.
[18]*William Frey, "Millennial and senior migrants follow different post-recession paths," Brookings Institution, 2013*, Retrieved from http://www.brookings.edu/research/opinions/2013/11/15-millennial-senior-post-recession-frey.
[19]*Megan Benetsky, Charlynn Burd, and Malanie Rapino, "Young adult migration: 2007–2009 to 2010–2012," US Census Bureau Report Number ACS-31, March 18, 2015*, Retrieved from http://www.census.gov/library/publications/2015/acs/acs-31.html.

Great Recession. Ever since 2007, the number of Millennials who moved has been less than the previous generations at similar ages.

Not interested in cars?

There have been many surveys that have revealed that Millennials have a low preference for vehicle ownership. Leases overtook automobile purchases as the preferred way to buy a car. Trading one every several years is the preferred path to vehicle acquisition.

Core Characteristics of Millennials

To be straightforward, Millennials seem to be the hardest demographic to understand. They have an ever-changing consumption of online media. Their trends and sentiments alter all the time toward online advertising. They could even be referred to as "the motion generation." To successfully market to Millennials, advertisers tend to try and figure their current behaviors out. Once they understand how Millennials think, it is easier to create advertisements that speak to them. With that being said, let us look at some of the things that marketers look at when creating advertisements for Millennials.

Millennials are focused on saving

Although Millennials have strong buying power, which is a mixture of the mounting debt they are in and their income, they still earn 20% less than what their parents did at this point in their lives. A millennial between the ages of 25-34 currently has an average annual salary of $40,000. In fact, not only do they make lesser money, but they also own less property compared to their parents. They lean more toward renting properties and cars than buying these essentials. Therefore, in attempts to combat the lower-income they have, more Millennials have their focus on building up savings. According to research[20], "one in six Millennials have already saved $100,000."

---

[20]*How much Should Gen X and Millennials have saved?* Retrieved from
https://www.forbes.com/sites/davidrae/2018/04/30/gen-x-Millennials-should-have-saved/#3e1131f02bd3

While they still have to work to establish a savings cushion that is comfortable enough, this does indicate that wisely spending money and saving is important to Millennials. Marketers attract Millennials by creating ads that speak to their desire to save. These ads must evoke feelings of responsibility, financial security, and self-reliance if they want to sit well with Millennials. Marketers know that Millennials have little or no interest in accumulating stuff for the sheer purpose of doing so; their mindset is set on long-term goals. Therefore, they show care when they spend, ensuring that they reach that long-term savings goal.

Millennials read blogs and reviews before they buy

Since information is more readily available now than it was ever before, people have multiple ways to educate themselves on any product they plan to purchase. Millennials conduct sufficient research before they go ahead with buying. In fact, research[21] has shown that 23% of Millennials claim that they like to research before purchasing anything. One of the reasons they spend their sweet time researching is because of the countless hours they spend online. It has been known that while 68.9% of Millennials use their phones to read product reviews, almost 80%[22] of them use phones to research prices.

This is not all. 33% of Millennials have reported having a preference for reading blog posts[23] before buying anything vs. 3%, who said that they prefer advertising in its traditional form – like TV and magazines. *"Millennials, on the whole, are not impulse-shoppers. They like to research, feel confident that the retailer and brand align with their values, and want to make sure they're getting the best price for an item, so they leverage a lot of channels to find this information."*

---

[21]*How Retailers Will Have to Adapt to Millennials' Spending Habits in 2018* Retrieved from https://www.gobankingrates.com/saving-money/savings-advice/Millennials-spending-habits-retailers/#4
[22]*Millennials, how they shop, and why they buy* Retrieved from https://www.herosmyth.com/article/millennial-consumer-how-they-shop-why-they-buy
[23] *Ten new findings about the millennial consumer* Retrieved from https://www.forbes.com/sites/danschawbel/2015/01/20/10-new-findings-about-the-millennial-consumer/#6233e4bf6c8f

Millennials look to their network for recommendations

At least 91% of Millennials are known to buy things based on recommendations from their friends. When you are scrolling through your Facebook feed, it is not uncommon to find it full of ads and promotional content. More often than not, people tend to scroll right past it and do not even spend a second reading or clicking on it. When it comes to Millennials, they stop when they see that their friends and family have posted about some restaurant or brand, for that matter. Their interest automatically rises, and they stop scrolling to find out more.

To reach them through this avenue, marketers incorporate referral marketing in their social media content. Compared to standard Facebook ads, Millennials are likelier to be receptive to this method of marketing. First, they find out who their customer advocates are. They are people who have used their products and have had a positive experience. Marketers use them by asking them to refer that product to other people. In fact, they also do it through social media influencers who people look up to. In return, they complement a special set of discounts or offers with their network of family and friends.

Millennials are concerned about the health and environmental issues

It is not news that organic food sales are on the rise. By 2019, the health and wellness food market had grown by approximately $1.1 trillion. Consumers have been asking questions – they want to know more about what their food contains. The response from producer companies is offering Millennials healthier solutions. They like to research; thus, they spend a good chunk of their time online researching how natural, organic foods are beneficial. Additionally, they have also read about the impact that production and delivery have on the environment before they purchase anything. Marketers use Google ads that focus on keywords Millennials are searching for.

Marketing value experiences over physical products

Millennials, unlike their parents, tend to see shopping more as a social activity than an errand. Millennials who are online shoppers have a greater interest in the user experience, much more than buying the products. Those who go to physical stores enjoy window shopping, grabbing lunch, and spending quality time with their friends. The engaging and social aspects of shopping after that conclude that 78% of Millennials would prefer spending their money on experiences than coveted goods.

Insight into the Millennial Mind

With the assumptions about Millennials growing by the day, one thing generally agreed upon is that this generation is purpose-driven and entrepreneurial. If an advertiser wants to reach out to Millennials, they must understand how deep-rooted their desires to positively impact the world are. While almost all Millennials still hold the American Dream or achieving that 'good life' close to them, their dreams are now focused on multiple ideas.

They want to own their companies, be set free of their debts, and become incredibly wealthy too, for that matter. We have already shed light on how this generation, being as non-traditional as it is, has a unique way of looking at advertising. For instance, events like buying a home or getting married do not particularly resonate with Millennials.

Marketers Pay Attention to These Tips
Quality over Quantity

More and more trends have started to show that Millennials trust people who they respect. When taken into consideration as a whole, they tend to be more skeptical of different brands and all the messages they send out. Brands are encouraged to invest in high-quality and engaging events to meet their advertising needs. Advertisers must speak with those influencers that ultimately connect with modern consumers. When marketers seek this organic, systematic marketing approach, they easily reach Millennial consumers and motivate them to become advocates and supporters of their brands.

Deeper Immersion

In order to send out any message to the millennial generation, social media and technology are the way to go. Marketers use campaigns and creative/interactive content to fuse an artistic message using a social platform. In fact, some even go ahead and investigate a unique tech experience in the form of a multi-sensory device to stand out against the noise. The expected way of the future is virtual reality. Therefore, brands have really been using it to get to Millennials.

Social Responsibility

In successful branding, this is not a new role. Thanks to the progress of technology and social media, Millennials are more informed than ever. This is not a generation that shuts their eyes in the face of rising issues. They have a voice and are not afraid to use it against social vices. For issues like equality, sexuality, or obesity, they have a growing concern. Thus, when marketing to them, brands ensure they are more "woke" and sensitive to these issues, as they plan, develop, and produce any type of content.

Listen to the Conversation

Now more than ever, it has become easier to stay informed of what the Millennials converse about. Advertisers make sure they keep a tab on the latest trends and wishes of this generation through their social media. They track bloggers and sign up for alert systems, all to see what is trending. Geo-tracking, geo-fencing, and keyword tracking are all very prevalent ways to track these consumers and their conversations. How many of us have googled a subject or texted something to suddenly see an advertisement minutes later appear in our social media feed?

Make it Authentic

Time and time again, I have emphasized on this one fact about Millennials: they want connection. They do not care about the quality or quantity of a product.

They care about how it makes them feel. They do not want to feel marketed to or sold to, or blatantly advertised. They want to discover brands on their own terms. Therefore, marketers have a different way to approach a campaign directed to Millennials. They think about how advertisers' products and services can complement their habits, lifestyles, and passions. These people love stories, and creativity is what keeps them engaged. Brands tend to lean toward establishing an emotional connection with this audience to shine among other brands.

Not an Easy Undertaking

It all comes down to one thing – marketing to Millennials is not a small task. Their interests are diverse, and at the end of the day, advertisers must carefully study the group of Millennials they plan to target to do so effectively. While the majority of their marketing is done online, traditional media sources should not be forgotten at the same time. In a fast-paced world, marketing is always evolving. However, as long as traditional media is used in conjunction with social media, it can be effective, too. Millennials are a generation that is quite successful. Therefore, it is important to inspire them before doing anything else.

Chapter 11: Gen Z – How Are They Different and How Advertisers Communicate To Them

If anything, you must know by now that as generations evolve, marketers need to step up their game. For every targeted generation, the advertisements have to be specific to them so that it works out effectively. More often than not, people talk about Millennials and what makes them tick, or how they should be marketed to. It causes people to forget that another generation has also come after them. Consequently, the marketing focus must shift to them. And, this shift will need to be transformative and disruptive. Considering the historical pattern of how advertisements have shaped over the years, advertisers need to change their approach to targeting Gen Z.

Gen Z is the generation that was born after 1996. There are 3 billion of them worldwide, which represents 35% of the global population. This "mobile first" generation represents $143 billion dollars in spending power, a significant market that should command attention from brands, advertisers and sponsors.

According to the leading Gen Z creator company Zebra IQ, this group is a video-first generation. Over 65% of Gen Z prefers FaceTime to keep in touch with friends. Mobile video and video chatting while multi-tasking is easy for Gen Z, while its downright debilitating for other generations. Zebra IQ founder Tiffany Zhong states that Gen Z is an "ironic, emoji-driven messaging generation." You'll find this generation direct messaging on gaming platforms such as Twitch, YouTube, Fortnite, Discord and others. Making new contacts by sharing memes and trending content and taking part in exclusive experiences is top of mind.

Advertisers can create authentic experiences and have authentic conversations with this elusive, hard to reach demographic by building immersive experiences and meeting them where they live and play. For Gen Z, more often than not, means esports. As an example, Fortnite is building immersive experiences within their platform. In April 2020 they presented an in-game concert from leading American rapper, Travis Scott. Scott's first three solo albums all went platinum and his third LP, 2018's Astroworld gave him his first number-one debut on the Billboard 100. By creating an in-game immersive experience for Fortnite players, Epic Games delivered 27.7 million unique views, and 45.8 million total views. At the peak of the 2020 pandemic lockdown, this virtual and immersive experience delivered an engaged audience and entertainment for a starved population which was living without live concerts, sports, theater, or in-person bars and dining.

Gen Z also highly values their privacy and wants to be able to control who sees their content, even on a person by person basis. This control enables them to present their personas via multiple social platforms and means that advertisers cannot just buy bulk Facebook ads like they do for other generations and expect to reach this group. Smart advertisers and sponsors are aligning with companies like Epic Games and their popular Fortnite game to create unique experiences that draw in the audience, instead of shotgun blasting out a branding message.

Also, Gen Xers and Millennials are expected to inherit as much as $68 Trillion dollars from Baby Boomers over the next several decades. A great wealth transfer will soon be upon us as the younger generations will inherit trillions of dollars from the "Boomers." Millennials are already predicted to be the first generation to be worse off than their parents in terms of earning power and wealth creation, so this boost in their bottom-line wealth will be welcome and much needed. (Thanks, Mom and Dad!)

This situation of being worse off isn't for lack of participating in the promise of the system.

According to a report from Pew Research Center, 39% of millennials aged 25-37 have a bachelor's degree or higher compared to 35% of baby boomers. Yet millennials have 41% less wealth than a similarly aged adult in 1989. Therefore, this great wealth transfer from boomer to millennials and Gen Z will likely be transformational in the life of many in the younger generations. Obviously, that only increases the buying power of this sector.

When you take the first glance, you might think Gen Z and Millennials are quite similar. However, the subtle differences between the two generations become more apparent only when you take a more in-depth look. It is these little, seemingly insignificant differences that are quite important to marketers. Let's discuss how advertisers must tweak their approach to attract this, the youngest generation.

Reaching the Gen Z Audience

Even though Gen Zers have quite the reputation as arduous individuals, advertisers can still successfully use different methods to sell their products or services to them. Whenever discussing the market reach of this generation, every marketer should keep one thing in mind. This is a generation of well-informed and arguably opinionated people. Among other things, brands that earn their loyalty as customers really speak to them in genuine and authentic ways. An interesting fact is that this trait is unique to this generation only. The previous generations were more bent on caring more about the quality of the product that they consumed. That brings us to the question of *how brands can advertise in a way to earn their loyalty?* The answer is much simpler than one would presume it to be. To give a sense of reliability to Gen Z, sell an all-encompassing brand and its enthralling story by embedding itself in the places and platforms where they live their lives.

Authenticity

One word that should be kept in mind at all times is authenticity when thinking of ways to best reach this demographic. According to research[24], at least 63% of Gen Zers want their marketing to be done by "real people" instead of celebrities. For many generations, people have been impressed by celebrities, wanting to follow their trends, and so on. This new generation, on the other hand, only care about originality. They see through the masks celebrities wear and relate more to "real people." They would rather view a grainy, shaky video clip with bad lighting shot on an iPhone with a sincere message, than a slickly

---

[24]*Deep Focus' Cassandra Report: Gen Z Uncovers Massive Attitude Shifts Toward Money, Work and Communication Preferences* Retrieved from
https://www.globenewswire.com/news-release/2015/03/30/1308741/0/en/Deep-Focus-Cassandra-Report-Gen-Z-Uncovers-Massive-Attitude-Shifts-Toward-Money-Work-and-Communication-Preferences.html

produced and polished professional video. This has given rise to the "influencer" phenomenon.

Influencers are real people who build tremendous numbers of followers on social platforms through becoming credible spokespersons for brands . People resonate more with influencers who have a couple of thousand followers because they see them as an every-day person. They prefer them over celebrities because they believe that these people are only part of the audience, and do not belong to some huge corporate manipulation. Since they follow influencers because they are genuinely interested in their lives, they consider them more authentic, and thus trust their opinions more than actors and other celebrities.

Keep it Succinct

When marketers found that millennials have an attention span of 12 seconds, they were quite baffled. Then came Gen Z with an average attention span of only 8 seconds. The most popular uploaded video clips on the app sensation Tik Tok are limited to 15 seconds. What does that tell marketers? They must come up with a storytelling approach to get their message across and make an impact, but everything should happen within eight seconds. The hard part is not cracking the code of how to effectively reach out to Gen Zers (hint: through selling them your heartfelt and authentic story). Instead, it is about finding an effective way of reaching out. They often do it through Instagram, Tik Tok, or Snapchat stories, where ephemeral content is used to make quick advertisements. You see, Gen Z, although different from other generations in many ways, is not that hard to engage with. Marketers just have to be strategic and approach them differently.

In the age of the ever-changing internet, targeting a generation is unlike any other. Gen Z does not remember a time when the internet did not exist, and as such, it's not surprising to learn that over half of all Gen Z spends ten hours a day or more connected online, and 75% watches YouTube for at least two hours a day.

Marketers must learn the art of short-form writing and content creation. While older generations despise acronyms and new phrases, Gen Z is quite the opposite. They enjoy visually appealing content like memes, emojis, and gifs.

They also appreciate brands that speak to them in the same lingo they use, being well aware of the cultural references.

Keep Reaching Out/Retargeting

There is an abundance of information in today's world. This is why a company needs to authentically brand to keep this generation engaged to stay on top of their minds. This is only possible through online retargeting. Once someone from this demographic purchases a brand's product, they want to observe that the brand cares about them. When brands retarget their existing customers, not only do they stay relevant, but they also make them loyal brand advocates. And as we have learned, advocates become influencers. In a generation obsessed with instantaneous moments, impulsive decisions, and very fast-paced life, marketers must repeatedly reinforce their brand. Otherwise, fickle Gen Z with the micro-attention span can quickly forget them.

With that being said, it is also crucial not to overdo it. Advertisers must know and understand that while online retargeting is powerful, it may fatigue the buyers if brands push too hard. Thus, markets must always put a cap on their retargeting frequency because this demographic of people do not hesitate to lose interest. If they even slightly feel like they are being pushed or sold to, they step back because it is the opposite of caring and authenticity, which they expect and demand from a brand.

Corporate Social Responsibility

Generation Z cares much about the environment and socially responsible issues that directly affect their lives, so brands who promote a positive social or environmental impact really appeal to them. Most, if not all, people of this generation spend much time online disconnected from the real world around them, making it seem as though they lack character or substance. However, this is not true at all as they sincerely want to vocalize their beliefs and have a tendency to express their values online and in particular in their purchase decisions. Therefore, when a brand does the same, they feel connected to it, increasing that brand's appeal. Marketers must know that in order to pique the interest of this demographic, they should stay in the loop with everything happening around the world. Voicing inclusivity, sustainability, social injustice, and talking about relevant matters are essential for this generation. This has a huge impact on whether this generation finds a brand worthy or not.

Since this generation does not care much about the traditional ways of marketing, a brand needs to keep an active social media presence to keep them connected. They typically have a holistic standpoint through which they look at a brand before deciding whether they want to become customers. Thus, brands need to hop on the social media bandwagon to communicate their progressive values and then stay on top.

Engagement

One of the other unique things about this generation is their love for realness above everything. Therefore, they prefer any company that is upfront about what it values holistically and shows everything it has to offer. Brands or influencers that present a very real, warts and all version of themselves instead of a carefully polished version get the most engagement. Gary Vaynerchuck, known to his followers simply as Gary Vee, is the founder and Chairman of VaynerX and Vayner Media, a media and communications holding company and a power influencer with 8.8 million Instagram followers. Gary makes no excuses for presenting himself as real and as authentically as possible. He is known for his prolific cursing and no BS advice to the younger generation on the value of entrepreneurship and the power of social media, and the waste that he believes a formal college education is. This type of messaging resonates in a very powerful way with Gen Z.

Since technology has always been at their fingertips, they conduct research before purchasing. Marketers must ensure that they engage with Gen Z in a way that the connection created with them does not feel contrived. This is why it's tricky to market to them: one move can make or break a brand's reputation. Additionally, these people take the whole "first impression is the last impression" quite seriously. So, if the initial point of contact goes well, they are likelier to make a purchase. For a company to succeed, they need to market and advertise not just in the beginning but all the way till the end, so these people keep coming back, developing a long-term relationship.

Embrace a Messaging Shift

Brands have become accustomed to the messaging preferred by Millennials over the last few years. They expound on ideas like life is about risk-taking, and life experiences, and job-hopping as the new professional normal, which Millennials believe in. Since they are so close to Gen Z in age, also having grown with similar exposure to technology, people fall into this misconception that there has to be an overlap between their values. That is not the case, though. In fact, a recent poll[25] that compared the two generations found out that their views on numerous subjects were quite the opposite.

Gen Zers are more likely to seek stability and security in their jobs and finances and less likely to have risk-taking behavior. Gen Z is possibly one of the most practical generations, valuing things like stable jobs and saving money. Moreover, only 38% of them believe it is essential to have a proper work-life balance as compared to nearly half of millennials. They also tend to care more about their personal income and accomplishing personal financial goals. Thus, marketers must change their messages accordingly to target this generation better.

The Millennials versus Generation Z

According to the website, VisualCapitalist.com, there are some specific differences between Millennials and Gen Z.

- Millennials were raised by Baby Boomer, and Gen Z was raised by Gen X

- Millennials grew up during an economic boom, Gen Z during a recession

- Millennials focus on having life experiences, Gen Z focuses on saving money

---

[25] *The Value of CX: Why We Need To Start Talking About NPS Again* Retrieved from https://www.visioncritical.com/gen-z-versus-millennials-infographics/

- Millennials prefer brands that share their values, Gen Z prefer brands that feel authentic

- Millennials tend to be idealistic, Gen Z pragmatic

- Millennials were mobile pioneers, Gen Z are digital natives

- Millennials prefer Facebook and Instagram, Gen Z prefers Snapchat and Tik Tok

According to Inc.com, these are the following characteristics of Gen Z in society and in the workplace.

- They make up 25.9% of the U.S. population

- 49% identify as non-white (compared to 44% of Millennials, 40% of Gen X, and 28% of Boomers)

- 50% are connected online for 10 hours per day

- 98% own a smartphone

- 92% have a digital footprint

- 70% watch more than two hours of YouTube a day

- 40% say they are addicted to their phones

- 80% feel anxious and distressed when kept away from their personal electronic devices

- 72% prefer face-to-face conversations in the workplace

- 77% expect to work harder than previous generations

- 75% want to have multiple roles in an organization

- 36% say that equality is the most important cause they want their employer to support

- 72% believe racial equality is the most important issue today

Brands: Show You Care About Gen Z

The bottom line is that this is an audience that needs to know that the brands they care about also care about them and not just their success. As long as these customers are happy and feel cared for, they will stay loyal to a brand.

At the same time, brands need to know that there is another side to the story. One which is slightly different. Although the aforementioned marketing strategies are practical, and marketers use them to target this demographic, they are also known for staying a step ahead of brands. A short example can be taken by analyzing influencers. A business may spend a good amount of money creating a deal with influencers to market their product but may find it ineffective as these people might find new influencers to follow, and the old ones fade in popularity just as fast.

The truth is that even if currently modern brands can pull off blanket marketing, in 5 to 10 years, they will no longer be able to do so. The uniqueness of this generation is unmatched. Every member treasures their personal identity. Every member creates their own digital brand. Generalization is not the key; personalization is.

That brings one to the question; *what should brands do?* The answer is that to achieve a more personalized and one-to-one marketing relationship with this generation, smart brands are scrambling to leverage new technologies. It is ultimately a race to see who can be more innovative. Thus, brands are investing in different technologies like conversational interfaces, geo-tracking, advanced web cookies, SMS text and direct messaging, RFID bracelets, artificial intelligence, in-store beacons, and even drones. They do all of this to easily collect user data to personalize their individual experiences accordingly. The more data you have, the more personalized the message can become. The disruption to the market is that marketers are now required to have individual, personalized conversations with each potential customer, instead of generalized branded messaging to large sectors of demographic groupings.

Interestingly enough, this is not something that is only limited to being theoretical. Personalization is finally being made a reality. While there is not much objective data to support this idea, there was a recent study[26] of CMOs from the U.K., U.S, and China from organizations that had over $500 million in revenue. They found that at least two-thirds of these brands believe that in the near future, AI will play a crucial role in their companies. Firms who fail to follow this trend and do not use AI effectively will consequently fall behind and fail to engage customers in more relevant and personalized ways. They will miss out on data-driven insights that have a direct impact on sales and products. And when it pertains to esports and gaming, where and when are we going to see the intersection of artificial intelligence and traditional gaming?

Smart brands learn from the behaviors of an individual user and use them to tailor their experiences in a way nobody did before. They create "anticipatory" experiences on behalf of users, decided based on their behavior, preferences, and goals. An easy example to relate better to this is how Spotify makes customized playlists for every user called "Made Just For You."

In a nutshell, smart brands learn from every customer interaction and personalize it based on that data, wherever the customer is. Marketers provide Gen Z with a single connected and personalized experience and understand the emotional and rational dimensions of their journeys.

Using esports as a Marketing Tool

When marketing to this generation, another effective way is through leveraging authentic experiences in esports. From a marketing and advertising point of view, it is an exciting industry due to its rising impact on the society and the fact that it has now become a huge part of modern subculture on a global level. By now, it must be clear that esports has a booming following. More importantly, since all interactions happen online, esports viewership can be tracked with ease. Additionally, we have already established that targeting Gen Z is trickier than one would think. Yet, the majority of the esports audience includes Millennials and Generation Z and offers excellent marketing opportunities.

---

[26]*AI-READY OR NOT: ARTIFICIAL INTELLIGENCE HERE WE COME!* Retrieved from
http://www.webershandwick.com/uploads/news/files/AI-Ready-or-Not-report-Oct12-FINAL.pdf

Brands are given the opportunity to use an authentic channel that their audience trusts by reaching out to them through esports. Just the fact that brands are meeting them at their point of passion gives a company a leg up on credibility. Major non-endemic, advertising brands such as Intel, Mercedes, Pepsi Mountain Dew, Comcast Infinity, Disney, and the US Air Force are making big bets on esports sponsorships.

The fact of the matter is that due to being online on different social platforms for prolonged periods, this generation is desensitized to huge volumes of content spamming their social media. When brands sponsor through esports, they are equipped with the advantage to access their audience organically on their favorite channels. Shoutcasters are esports commentators who help brands get an opportunity to reach niche audiences. Since their followers are loyal and trust their opinions, brands can use these people as their ambassadors.

Esports is an ever-growing market. We have already expounded upon its growth patterns throughout the years. It is common for gamers to interact with game brands they like the most, even outside the game itself, by creating various channels where advertisers can reach them. To complement their in-game experiences, they tend to download companion apps. They spend a lot of time in viewing content that is on game-brand sites, and they also watch a lot of esports replay and tutorial videos on sites like Twitch.

In earlier chapters, we discussed different platforms where people watch esports, like Twitch. However, there are more popular destinations for gamers, such as Google-owned YouTube. In fact, even Yahoo launched its own esports website. Sports channels like ESPN now broadcast esports events, while the owners of traditional pro-sports teams are also making investments in esports teams.

Jonathan Sumers, who is the Senior Director of Esports Operations at the Cleveland Cavaliers NBA2K team says that two of the most important trends in esports are the growth of mobile gaming and the league model. As mobile gaming continues to grow, developers increasingly account for this shift to reach their target audience. The formation of leagues around larger titles is a reflection of the growth of esports to align with 'traditional' sports. This will enhance regional interest and excitement while giving more gamers nationally an opportunity to root for a 'hometown' team.

The point of this discussion is that advertisers who are on the lookout for new ways to target this generation should place a big bet on esports.

To see this better with a good example, let us take Mountain Dew as a case study for starters. It launched a Game Fuel campaign by partnering with brands like Titanfall 2 and Call of Duty to offer codes on their bottles, which people could redeem in their games for boosts. On the other hand, Old Spice launched a three-day promotion on Twitch that invited viewers to control a man in the woods by typing suggestions into a chat. Consequently, they garnered millions of views.

There are basically three main ways brands can target Gen Z through esports.

Sponsor a Team

The value of sponsorship has been a proven marketing option, whether it comes to esports or traditional sports. A tried and tested tactic for spreading awareness of any brand is through sponsorship alignment. When using it as a strategy in esports, one must make the determination whether they should sponsor the league, game, sport, team, or player that naturally aligns with their brand. Brands should gain a deep understanding of the audience's affinities, so they can position their products better. When they sponsor a team, every single player or even supporter of the team is likely to check the brand out.

Sponsor an Event

There are times when sponsoring a team may not be appropriate. It could be a bad strategy or out of the brand's budget. As we discussed the importance of a brand to align with the right team or player, they must also do the same to identify the perfect event to market in. For example, Mountain Dew has always promoted this idea of "living on the edge."

Therefore, it marketed to people who play games like Call of Duty and was very successful because those gamers tend to seek such a lifestyle. Similarly, fans who like to play fighting games tend to be more interested in motorsports. Thus, a natural sponsor for an esports fighting game tournament could be a car company. Much like player and team sponsorships, a company can drive top-of-the-funnel awareness through sponsoring or hosting an event. Regardless of the marketing goals or strategies, these events can be incredibly effective.

Become Part of the Community

Growing gathering spots for Gen Z include Twitch and YouTube, which provide exceptional value for a brand's media dollar. If a brand is not yet ready to sponsor an entire team or event, it can start small by marketing through these community channels. This can provide them with a great opportunity to experiment with reaching the target audience through esports. The key is to identify the genre that best befits the brand, its product, and marketing goals. The content and messaging can be later adjusted to create a more compelling match.

You might wonder how big these communities are. YouTube reaches 1.5 billion logged-in users every month. Twitch, based primarily on the video game industry, reports 10 million daily active users and more than 22,000 members of the Twitch Partner program – partners who are looking forward to customer support at all levels. Each of these vehicles allows for highly targeted display or video ads. In addition, many channels and hundreds of shows on Twitch offer endless opportunities for media placement, product placement, or anything else your marketing team can imagine. And in 2020, technology giants Google, Facebook and Amazon announced cloud gaming platforms,namely, Google Stadia, Amazon Luna and Facebook Gaming.

Luna is advertised as a platform where you can play your favorite device on your favorite screens. As everyone knows, when Amazon enters a market there is ordinarily significant disruption that follows. And mobile gaming is coming on big time. To challenge continual upgrades and new console launches from the 800-pound gorillas Microsoft and Sony, Nintendo's Switch which is a mobile based console, was the top selling video console game for 24 straight months, with 68 million being sold globally.

I want to add that brands need to stay a little too connected and have high technological and digital capabilities and understanding of this generation to advertise to them effectively. Brands must stay authentic and communicate on the ground level about how crucial it is to bring value to the fans. As a brand, you should take into account all these things, and before taking any steps, you must analyze every little detail. Remember, this generation cares about experiences, so tell your story. Aim for their hearts! If you make a place in their hearts, they will give you preference and loyalty over others.

Chapter 12: The Advertising Pivot

Advertising is much more than just a 30-second flashy video trying to grab your attention in between breaks in your favorite TV show or as you are scrolling down your social media feed. It's also more than a clever slogan that makes you smirk. On average, humans have gone from being exposed to about 500 ads per day in the 1970s to as many as 5000[27] daily today. There are countless forms of advertisements. Simply put, it is the art of grasping public attention toward an idea, service, or goods by paying an identified sponsor. For any sort of advertising, there are three main objectives: inform, persuade, and remind.

To Inform

Advertisements are used to increase brand exposure and awareness in the target market. Through them, potential customers are informed about the brand and the products or services it offers. It is the first step in attaining business goals.

To Persuade

A prominent objective of advertising is persuading customers to perform a specific task. This task can be anything from trying products and services or buying them. It may include developing a likable attitude toward the brand, which helps form its image.

To Remind

Advertising has another essential objective, and that is to reinforce the brand message. The existing and potential customers need to be given reassurances about the brand's vision time and time again. Advertising reminds all stakeholders about the brand's outlook and potential.

---

[27] *Cutting through advertising clutter* Retrieved from
https://www.cbsnews.com/news/cutting-through-advertising-clutter/

Types of Advertising

Over the last couple of decades, advertisement trends have evolved and adapted to the technological revolution. The world has already shifted from traditional advertisement platforms such as newspapers and radio to digital marketing. Regardless of how much it has progressed, traditional advertising is still what people first think of when they talk about marketing or advertising.

Traditional Advertising

When we talk about traditional advertising, it includes the "usual" avenues like broadcast television, cable television, outdoor billboards, newspaper, or radio for media placement. The reason they are called "traditional" is that they are the pioneering ways of advertising. They can be set apart from the modern advertising options that include online and viral marketing initiatives. Different types of traditional advertisements are described below.

Newspapers

Ads that appear in newspapers are information-dense. Newspapers are well suited to present complex messages like pharmaceutical advertisements, which contain specific product information and usually a tremendous number of disclaimers. Moreover, they are much more cost-efficient than TV, radio, or billboards. Thus, they allow the advertiser to present detailed information at a low price. People who read newspapers are generally used to getting in-depth information from it anyway. Therefore, the ads fit into the style and do not go ignored. An additional benefit of using newspapers as a medium for advertisement is that the consumer can keep the ad for future reference or use. With that being said, trends are now changing. The younger generation and consumers do not really read newspapers. They choose to stay informed through the internet.

Magazines

Ads in magazines are specific. That is because every magazine has a particular audience, so most of the advertisements address readers who share those same interests. Magazines have a targeted nature, present images of good visual quality, and have high credibility. This makes them likelier to influence and reach the right audience.

Network TV

Mass audiences are attracted through network TV, thus making it the highest-exposure medium. Being a visual medium, it requires creativity because there the competition is tough. Through television advertisements, emotion and information can both be conveyed to the audience.

Radio

Back in the day, almost every person used to listen to the radio. Thus, it was quite popular with marketers. Advertisements played on the radio are cost-effective because the impact is almost as great as the average TV ad, yet the cost is much less. Commercial radio stations are paid by the advertisers, and in exchange, their commercial is played for the entire listening audience.

Billboards

If an advertiser wants to do marketing on a large scale at a low cost, billboard advertising is the way to go. Billboards are typically placed in high traffic areas, such as highways and city centers. It ensures that they reach the highest number of pedestrians and drivers. For a business to build brand awareness and broadcast to as many people as possible, billboard adverting is quite useful. Since billboards are generally in busy areas, they are likely to reach a high number of people as compared to other methods of marketing.

Benefits of Traditional Advertising

These ads are usually impactful and easy to understand. Passing by a huge billboard that is visually bold, without noticing it, is nearly impossible. A striking TV commercial comes when people are watching news or television in general, making it a part of their lives. This makes these ads not just entertaining but also easy to digest.

When a business chooses printed marketing as a form of advertising, it ensures permanence. If, for instance, they place an advert in a famous magazine, it will stay there for a long time. Lastly, something you see outside is generally more memorable than what you see on your phone. One of the reasons for that is when you are on your phone, there are countless distractions, and it's easy to forget what you just saw. Digital advertising is considered disposable as once you see the advertisement, it's then gone, so a marketer needs to continually renew the ads for the best impact. There's always something else that comes up when browsing. Some advertisements, like the ones announcing new smartphones or those that appear in the Super-Bowl, are anticipated by people. Thus, they stay in their minds longer than any random Instagram ad.

In earlier times, consumers didn't have many choices for where they got their content. Since there were only three major broadcast networks (ABC, NBC, and CBS and then eventually FOX), the natural result of this was significantly sized audiences, allowing advertisers the luxury of getting their message out large and wide all at once. In 1983, the most popular television show at the time, M.A.S.H. on the CBS network, aired the series finale to over 106 million people. The episode was so highly anticipated that 30-second advertising slots sold for $450,000 dollars, in 1983.

To put that viewership number in perspective, the highest-rated television program of 2020 was the Super Bowl, which drew an audience of 102 million viewers. Nearly forty years later, cable television fractured that network TV model, and online platforms and mobile content has fractured it even more. The old school advertising model of one message to many has been replaced with advertising where and when the audience is, not where and when you tell them to be.

Problems with Traditional Advertising

The first problem with advertising in a traditional manner is that it is costlier than digital advertising. The reason for that is that when you are doing things through a traditional route, many additional costs are involved. It includes expenses like the paper you print the flyers on, the distribution of materials, and so on. Additionally, the audience has little or no interaction with the content. It means much less engagement is promoted through these types of advertisements, as it is more geared toward delivering the information to the audience. By nature, information is broadcasted out to large audiences, and it is one-way communication; brand to consumer. People can't really share the advertisements with their friends or "like" it, they just see it and the impact ends there. Lastly, the effectiveness of your advertisements can't be measured either. Thus, you will never know which customers made purchases from your brand after seeing the advertisement – whether it was delivered to the right audience. In simple terms, the success of the marketing campaign can't be tracked. Additionally, starting with the millennial generation, advances in technology such as DVR's that skip commercials and services like Hulu, Netflix, and others that offer no commercials and allow viewers to binge-watch their shows has overtaken the habit of tuning into your favorite show at a specific time and day each week. The exception to that rule is still live sports. Events such as the NFL's Super Bowl still command enormous audiences that deliver eyeballs for the old school Madison Avenue types.

Digital Advertising

Another word for digital advertising would be online advertising. It is an advertisement in any shape or form that appears online, whether you are scrolling through your Instagram feed, playing before a YouTube video, or seeing it at the top of search results. Most, if not all, digital advertisement is paid. It offers countless benefits, such as diversity – you can precisely choose which ads are best for your customers and business. Considering what your brand has to offer, some platforms and methods will obviously be better suited for you than others.

How it Began

October 27th, 1994, was the day the advertising industry witnessed the emergence of digital advertising as one of the first banner ads appeared on HotWired.com. The ad was made for AT&T's virtual tour of the world's art museums; it was 468 by 60 pixels in size and said, *"Have you ever clicked your mouse right HERE? YOU WILL."* And so it began.

Digital Advertising Formats

There are various ad formats in the diverse digital advertising landscape. To create a new ad, one can also use an amalgamation of two ad categories. To remind your existing visitors to complete a purchase, remarketing can also be done with display ads. There are many types of digital ad formats. These are five of the most common ones.

Search Engine Marketing

When you open Google or Bing to search for anything, the search results come back with the tag 'Ad' at the top of the Search Engine Results Page. They appear as a result of search engine marketing. It is generally seen as the most commonly used ad format. In this type of marketing, competitors bid with one another on keywords to appear at the top of the page in search results. There are two types of SEM ads; either pay per click (PPC) or Cost Per Thousand Impressions (CPM). PPC means every time someone clicks on your ad, you have to pay. In CPM, regardless of the clicks, you pay for every 1,000 impressions on your ad.

Display Ads

As we already know, this is where ads began. These types of ads primarily use images and text. They appear on ad networks or search engines affiliated with ad networks. Video ads, banners, text, mobile, images, and pop-ups are the most common types of display ads.

Social Media Ads

Social media presents brands with a huge opportunity to advertise because a large audience spends a lot of time on social media. Platforms like Twitter, YouTube, Facebook, Instagram, LinkedIn, or Reddit can easily be used to promote products and brands. There are different ways social media ads can be used. For instance, in creating event attendees, generating leads, building a community, and boosting website conversations and app installations, among other things.

Native Advertising

Native ads are quite a clever way of advertising. They do not appear like typical ads. They are labeled under headings like 'Recommended Reading,' 'Related Stories,' or 'Promoted Stories.' They match the content that you are currently consuming. Only once you click on them, it redirects you to the advertiser's website. A variation of this is also referred to as "click-bait."

Remarketing

This is quite an exciting way of marketing. It is when a person checks out a particular product on any website and then moments later sees ads for it all over their social media feed. Another word for remarketing is retargeting. It uses website cookies to follow you on the web, ultimately getting a hold of your search patterns.

Why Digital Advertising Is Successful

In a nutshell, digital advertising is specific, affordable, and easy to use. Businesses choose to opt for this type of advertising because it provides them with a cost-effective strategy that is measurable and reaches audiences with the intensity and expanse they desire. There are quite a number of advantages.

Reaches Target Audience

While marketing, if a business chooses to purchase a billboard and advertise through it, it can be challenging to measure its true impact. There is no guarantee that people who view it will make the buying decision. In fact, one can argue that most of the viewers wouldn't even be the targeted audience. A digital ad campaign, on the other hand, is literally the opposite of that. Digital advertising allows the targeting of people who actually have an interest in your products and services. They can be easily located using interests, location, and purchase/searching behavior. Additionally, it is a smart way of advertising because audiences are being reached out to when they are already searching for a product in the industry where a certain business operates.

Affordable

There is no specific size a company needs to be to benefit from digital advertising. It can be as small as a home business, or a single real estate agent or as big as a massive corporate enterprise. When compared to traditional advertising, this kind of marketing allows businesses to create their own budget. To launch a billboard or air a television commercial, you have to work with the established costs and norms in the industry. With digital ads, you can decide how much you want to spend and whom to specifically target with your marketing.

Strategic and holistic

Whether a business is advertising online or offline, they like to have options and a good strategy. A brand can launch its ads through various platforms like Google, YouTube, Instagram, Facebook, and so on. Digital advertising can be used by a company for reaching a variety of goals, including driving product sales, promoting brand awareness, getting an increment in contact requests, and much more.

Instant Results

One of the most significant perks of digital media advertising is the fact that results can be instantly expected. As soon as a company launches its online paid campaign, it starts to reach new audiences, get phone calls, orders, and more. What's more, is that these actions can be easily tracked and associated with marketing campaigns. With efficient tracking, it is easy for a company to see the impact of its digital advertising campaigns.

Four definitive bidding models in digital advertising

Now that we have explored the different formats of digital advertising, it is crucial to understand what different bidding models of online digital marketing are available. The four most common bidding models used are enlisted below:

Cost-per-click (CPC)

Every time someone clicks on the ad a business has put up online, they must pay for it. Marketers often choose to go through with CPC because they do not pay for someone to view their ad, but only to interact with it. One click and the user is redirected to the business's website. Different platforms that use CPC include Google Ads, Twitter, Facebook, Bing Ads, and more.

Cost-per-thousand-impressions (CPM)

When a company's ad earns 1000 views or impressions, they must pay. While it is widely known for building brand awareness for huge brands like Coca-Cola or Pepsi, small scale businesses can't benefit much from it because it is not quite cost-effective. They have to pay for views, not interaction, and that does not necessarily translate into measurable actions like purchases. CPM is available on the same platforms as CPC.

Cost-per-lead (CPL)

Every time your ad generates a new lead, the business has to pay. It is important for the business to develop an ad that attracts and targets high-quality users. Otherwise, they will have to pay the same amount for low-quality leads. A few examples of platforms offering CPL are Google Ads and Facebook.

Cost-per-action (CPA)

In this, a company pays when the user completes a desired action. This action inculcates a range of conversions from purchasing a specific product to signing up for an email newsletter. While companies generally use this option to reach out on social media, they can also benefit from it on different channels like searching.

Disadvantages of digital marketing
They can be annoying

Sometimes people only want to scroll through their social media feed without being interrupted by any sponsored ads. This may create a dislike for the brand.

High competition

While global audiences can be reached through digital marketing, there is also a global competition on the same hand. It can be challenging to be unique enough to stand out against competitors and make an impact.

Less permanent

The truth is that while they may be effective in various ways, they can also have a fleeting, temporary character. Being intangible, they are likely to be easily ignored. It takes one click for the audience to go onto a new page, and your ad is gone from their screen.

Constantly evolves

Much like everything else, digital marketing keeps evolving, and there is always a lot to learn. New technologies such as ad-blocking software eliminate advertisements from a user's feed, negating the ability to reach the consumer. Robo-clicks and the inability to measure "real" and engaged viewers from computer-generated robo-users make the marketer's job of measuring the ROI tremendously difficult. From search engine marketing to social media, every channel needs its specialist to get the most benefits out of it.

Conclusion

Every single thing comes with a set of pros and cons. There is never a perfect way to do something. There is not just one road a person can take to reach a particular destination or achieve a specific goal. There are always different ways and routes. The fact of the matter is that with all the great things about traditional marketing, it has become a little outdated. But at the same time, its permanence and stronger impact are things that digital marketing lacks. The two types of marketing do not have to be pages of different books.

They can and should, by all means, support one another and go hand in hand. There is no rule book that reinstates that if a brand is using one type of advertisement, they cannot use the other. Sure, you must know that some things are genuinely outdated, for instance, radio ads, but that is not the entirety of traditional marketing. One can also use it in the form of billboards or brochures – things people are more likely to see. The printed ads can have the link to that brand's social media – this way, it can turn into a two-way interaction, too.

Brands should be more open-minded and holistic when it comes to advertising. There is no right or wrong, or some sort of all-in or nothing approach. A multi-channel approach means that you are efficient by making use of the power and benefits that come with both options. You enjoy the reach of traditional methods and also the convenience and accessibility of digital platforms. When a company is deciding whether they want to market online or offline, they must remember that they will both offer specific individual results. Both methods are better together because not everyone is always online or using their phones; that is where the gap is filled with traditional marketing. The key is diversity.

Chapter 13: Influencers

*"There are exceptional people out there who are capable of starting epidemics. All you have to do is find them." -**Malcolm Gladwell***

If there was any doubt that there is big money is esports, all you have to do is look at the flurry of big name esports athlete signings at the end of 2020.

TSM (Team SoloMid) signed Hu Shuo-Chieh, known professionally as "Sword Art" to a two-year contract that will pay him $6 million for 2021 and 2022, giving the professional "League of Legends" player what is believed to be the richest salary in the LCS and among any esports team based in North America. The guaranteed deal for Sword Art eclipses the previously reported high of Dignitas's deal of $2.3 million over two years for Heo Seung-hoon, known as "Huni".

TSM (Team SoloMid) is a professional esports organization based in the U.S. TSM fields players in the League of Legends, Apex Legends, Valorant, Heathstone, Super Smash Brothers, and Fortnite among others making them the Dallas Cowboys of esports. TSM founder, Andy Dinh, has stated that he thinks that TSM will one day become the Dallas Cowboys, Real Madrid and F.C. Barcelona combined. He says that his investment thesis is that teams that win, build dollars down the road, creating a legacy and a large fan base of consistency and winning. (SOURCE = WASHINGTON POST.COM. 11/26/2020)

One of the most important trends has been the rise in influencers. The fact that social media has been on a meteoric rise is certainly not breaking news. Ultimately, with that came the rise of social media influencers! I know that I have mentioned influencers a few times throughout this book, and you probably have an idea of who an influencer is. However, for those people who may still be a little confused, let's take a deep dive and explore it in greater detail.

Typically, social influencers are people equipped not only with knowledge but also experience in their industry. They voice their opinions, review products, and give out valuable recommendations to their audience. Due to the strong relationship with their audience, they can affect their purchasing decisions.

Brands should know that they are not just mere marketing tools but assets that allow brands to build social relationships and achieve marketing objectives.

Types of Influencers

While the word influencer is quite dismissive on its own, its branches spread out far. There are quite a few categories of influencers, each having further subsets. They can be separated in various ways, for instance, by numbers, types of content, level of influence, the niche they operate, and so on. This means that while some may appear "low" in a particular category, they may have a more substantial impact when looked through a different lens.

For instance, many mega-influencers are also celebrities. While they have a huge fan following, they may exercise very little influence on the audience they target because they are not specific content experts. While on the other hand, some micro and nano-influencers are likely to impact others profoundly in their dedicated niche. This makes them a more significant asset for a company than the former. Let us look at the different ways we can categorize influencers.

By Follower Numbers
Mega-Influencers

These are people with a massive number of followers on different social media platforms. While there is no hard and fast rule on the exact number of followers that separates one category of influencers from another, mega influencers are generally people with at least one million followers on one of their social networks. While some mega-influencers have gained their vast following through different online activities, most of them are movie stars, sports stars, musicians, or reality television stars who gained their fame offline. Their services are quite expensive, with up to $1 million per post. They often have agents working on their behalf. Therefore, they are usually approached only by major brands.

Macro-Influencers

These people are one step away from being mega-influencers. They are more accessible as influencer marketers. Their followers range from somewhere between 40,000 to one million. There are two types of people in this category, the first being grade B celebrities who haven't gotten their big break yet. The latter are successful online experts who have worked their way to the top and built a stronger community following as compared to other influencers. The latter are also the ones who are more useful for firms wanting to engage in influencer marketing.

Generally, these people have an excellent profile. Therefore, they are great for raising awareness. Since they are greater in numbers, brands can easily find a suitable one for their branding and marketing needs. Additionally, they often communicate directly instead of relying on agents, making it easier to reach out to them. One crucial thing to note here is that some of these people also purchase their followers, committing influencer-fraud. Hence, before reaching out to one, brands should do their research.

Micro-Influencers

Micro-influencers are simply regular people who are known for their knowledge of a specialized niche. They often gain a small but highly specific audience that is devoted to some product, service, or theory. Their level of influence is not defined by their number of followers but by the close relationship they have with them. Generally, they are people with followers ranging from 1000 to 40,000. The one thing about this category of influencers is that they usually value the relationship they have with their audience a lot and stand for what they believe in. They are one of them and are embraced as one of us. Thus, if they do not believe that a particular brand is good enough or not appropriate for their audience, they will not take up the offer regardless of monetary benefits. These influencers have been gaining more and more fame lately to the point where they may even be called "traditional celebrities" when it comes to Generation Z. It is mainly because of how genuine and authentic they are – traits that the Gen Z demographic cares about the most.

Nano-Influencers

These are the newest types of influencers who may have less than a thousand followers, but they are usually highly specialized. Their followers are interactive. They could be seen as a proverbial big fish in a very small pond. Their followers really care about their opinions and are interested in what they have to say. For brands that make highly specialized and niche products tailored to a specific market, they are the way to go. With that being said, since they have a small following but strong influence, a brand may have to work with scores of such influencers if they want to reach a broad audience.

By Types of Content
Bloggers

The most authentic and active relationship with their fans is generally held by micro-bloggers, and lately, they are being recognized by brands too. For some time now, blogging and influencer marketing have been interlinked. Many highly influential blogs are operating on the internet. Consequently, the minute your product or service gets a positive review from them, it can lead to their supporters wanting to give it a shot too. If there is an influential and well-followed blog, a brand may even be able to purchase a sponsored post on their page. This allows that influencer to write a post on your behalf.

YouTubers

Brands often collaborate with popular YouTube content creators, who promote their products or services on their YouTube channel. Instead of having an entire website, content creators often make a YouTube channel and create a fan-following through it.

Tik Tok'ers

To describe Tik Tok as Twitter or Instagram with video, totally short-changes the explosive rise in popularity of this platform. Tik Tok, with very brief videos of either 15 seconds or 60 seconds, has become a worldwide sensation. Content creators upload home-made videos that are too short for YouTube, and messaging that with just words alone wouldn't have the same resonance on Twitter or Facebook. And anyone can be a content creator! The pandemic of 2020 had a quarantined locked down audience thirsting for creative content and outlets. Television studios were shut down, so no new programming came out for months and months. Live sports took a long time to acclimate to this as well. Therefore, Tik Tok can now lay claim to being the new disrupter of the age. So what you're telling me is that there is a captive audience of people watching other people lip-sync to songs and comedy bits, or do choreographed dance routines in short bursts? YES! Just as there is an audience of gamers who love to watch other gamers play. Real people watching real people!

Podcasters

This is relatively a new form of online content and has been exponentially growing in popularity, and is finally seeing its monetization potential. Joe Rogan signed an exclusive deal with Spotify for his podcast, *The Joe Rogan Experience*. According to the Wall Street Journal, the multi-year deal is believed to be worth over $100 million dollars.

By Level of Influence
Celebrities

For as long as anyone can remember, celebrities have been the original influencers. While their importance as influencers has started to fade out, they still have a role to play. Big brands still hire celebrities as brand ambassadors because, at the end of the day, most people still look up to them. For instance, brands like Nike and Adidas use famous soccer stars like Lionel Messi and Christiano Ronaldo to promote their new shoes or anything else. It results in all the sports enthusiasts wanting to purchase these goods immediately. Michael Jordan started the Nike craze with his branded "Air Jordan's." Everyone wanted to own a pair!

The truth is that only a small number of celebrities are willing to partake in this kind of influencer campaigns or have the gravitas to sway social opinions, which is why they are highly unlikely to be cheap. With that being said, if the product is something the celebrity already uses and likes, they may not mind using their influence to tell people how good they believe the product is. At the same time, the problem with using celebrities as influencers is that they cannot influence every type of audience and affect their buying patterns.

Key Opinion Leaders

Thought leaders such as journalists and industry experts are also excellent as influencers. Therefore, they hold an essential position for brands too. These people gain the audience's respect because of the position they hold or the qualifications and experience they have about their topic of expertise. More often than not, they have earned this respect because of their workplace's reputation or their exemplary performance or achievement. For instance, a journalist for the New York Times may not be an expert on every subject he writes on, but people respect him for being associated with such a prestigious publication. Such experts include journalists, industry experts, professional advisors, and academics.

If a company or brand grasps the attention of a journalist of a national newspaper, and they end up talking positively about that company, it may be equivalent to a huge social media influencer or blogger doing so. The catch here is that when a journalist does it, they do not charge any money for it to maintain the credibility of impartiality. One thing to denote is that these people may not have a large or active social following and only have a reputation in an offline setting.

People with Above Average Influence on Their Audience

The best influencers are often those who built their online reputation based on the fact that they are an expert in a certain niche. While they are similar to key opinion leaders, their reputation is gained informally through their social media use. The quality of the blogs they write, posts they make, videos they craft, or podcasts they deliver creates their reputation.

Influencers' Popularity with Gen Z

Throughout this book, I have emphasized the fact that Generation Z are digital natives and are the ones glued to their phones, ones that love authenticity and honesty. These two traits are found in influencers, and it is the reason they have a stronger impact than celebrities when it comes to this demographic. Gen Z is challenging to reach through traditional media channels like newspapers or television. It makes influencer marketing all the more important when it comes to targeting them. The sheer fact that this type of marketing allows brands to connect with young consumers has been driving them to spend more money on it. One forecast suggested a growth to $15 billion by 2022 from $8 billion last year in 2020.

According to a research study by Kantar[28], among Gen Z, Facebook is still the most popular social media application. Other research indicates that Instagram, owned by Facebook, is actually the most popular app for running influencer campaigns. *"Almost 80% of brands using the image-sharing app most frequently for influencer campaigns, making it more popular than Facebook (46%), YouTube (36%), Twitter (24%), and LinkedIn (12%), as per Influencer Marketing Hub. Instagram's role in the space has grown with its user base, which eMarketer forecasts will lift 5.4% to 112.5 million U.S. users this year."*

This generation is known to have an open mind to a vast range of influencers, with 87% of them saying that they follow at least one if not more influencers from a race or ethnicity different from their own, according to Kantar's study. Gen Z'ers are known to be social butterflies, relying widely on many social media apps, with 39% of them having at least four or more social media accounts compared to 15% of the general population who are users of that many social platforms. Additionally, according to Kantar's research, the popularity among social media apps in this generation are as follows: Facebook (62%), Instagram (55%), YouTube (54%), and Snapchat (52%). This is even before the advent of Tik Tok.

---

[28] *Gen Z relies on influencers for purchase decisions, Kantar says* Retrieved from https://www.mobilemarketer.com/news/gen-z-relies-on-influencers-for-purchase-decisions-kantar-says/573264/

Quite a lot of people wonder why Gen Z is so bent on responding to influencers. A research was conducted by The Influencer Market[29] in which young people were asked why they like to follow influencers. Their answers ranged from reasons like inspiration, aspiration, voyeurism, learning about new trends, and interesting, fun content. In some of their words:

"Seeing their successful lives inspires me to do better in my own."

"They are fun to watch, and it's close as I get to meet someone famous."

"They are more in tune with the things that I like, so I follow them to see the newest trends.

"They provide interesting content in a more personal setting."

Influencer Marketing

All of this points toward one thing over and over again... Generation Z is rooting for influencers, and brands can use this to their advantage through influencer marketing. Influencer marketing extends the reach of an existing influencer that has built an enormous following. A strong brand reputation in a particular niche can attract influencers to support your brand, endorse your brand, or re-create content, with the aim of increasing brand awareness and sales. With that being said, let us explore how brands can leverage this to their advantage.

Product Reviews

Customers find it challenging to trust products that blow their trumpets. Instead, they rely on recommendations from their friends, relatives, acquaintances, and, of course, the influencers they love. According to a research study, the influence of social media is the most effective and reliable source of driving sales. Therefore, partnering with influencers to create and upload a trusted product review is a great way to influence purchase decisions. It allows the promoter to share their experience, explaining the pros and cons of your

---

[29]*Why young Americans follow influencers* Retrieved from
https://morningconsult.com/wp-content/uploads/2019/11/The-Influencer-Report-Engaging-Gen-Z-and-Millennials.pdf

product. Such reviews are probably more reliable than the advertising that only shows how good your product is. This is an advantageous marketing strategy to convert and drive sales.[30]

For instance, the Sephora community is called "Beauty Insider." Its members are well-known beauty bloggers and social posters. They first use newly-launched Sephora products themselves before sharing their honest feedback. The community is renowned for its useful reviews and is incredibly popular in the beauty industry. Sephora customers love this real answer and rely more on the brand. It also leads to an increase in earnings and conversions. While reviews are helpful, unboxing videos are another way to create a buzz about a new product. By sending influencers a coupon code that customers use for a discount, these campaigns can be made more effective. The coupon code not only offers the buyer a discount courtesy of their favorite influencer, but it allows the brand to track ROI based on that particular influencer campaign.

Contests and Giveaways

A giveaway is a pretty straightforward and effective strategy to increase the engagement of the audience and boost the reach of certain content. Giveaways allow influencers to guide specific actions from their users, such as liking a certain post, tagging their friends, following the mentioned accounts, and so on. If, for example, the product of a certain brand is included in the giveaway and the audience is required to follow their social media account to enter the contest, it will give that brand a quick popularity boost. This is a swift and easy strategy that can help generate leads in the long run.

Social Media Takeover

Social media takeovers have been getting quite famous lately. During one, a company or brand allows a social influencer to take over their social media accounts for a designated time. One of the major advantages of this is that the audience is suddenly presented with unique and fresh content. Since influencers

---

[30]*The influence of influencers: new research unveiled* Retrieved from
https://www.gen.video/blog/the-influence-of-influencers-new-research-unveiled

are people whose expertise lies in creating user-centric content, it can boost audience engagement on the brand's page. It also gives your content credibility since people look at influencers as people who are trustworthy sources of valuable information.

Collaborate with Bloggers

When a brand is willing to collaborate with influential bloggers, they resultantly increase brand exposure in the process. The first step is finding influencers in their industry who would be willing to post on their behalf or promote their product or service. It helps promote the brand in the eyes of that influencer's loyal audience.

Do's and Don'ts to boost your influencer marketing

1. To maximize your marketing ROI, it is vital to establish the purpose of your marketing campaign.

2. Make sure the influencer is an expert from your niche.

3. Do not work with a powerful non-expert in your industry, as it can negatively affect your advertising campaign.

4. Always give someone creative freedom and encourage them to come up with ideas for an engaging campaign for your brand.

5. Give your products to the influencer and regularly ask them to share their honest and true feedback.

6. When planning any giveaway or competitions, be sure to clearly mention the guidelines for participating for your fans.

7. In capturing social media, do not confuse the influence of someone who does not fit your brand's identity and values.

8. Make sure you choose a website or social platform with a high domain worth publishing your guest post.

Conclusion

If it is not already quite clear, brands can and should use influencer marketing when trying to reach Generation Z. This demographic is unlike any other with their own set of values and rules, things that make them stand out among others. They do not follow the traditional ways of things, neither do they care about them. They are opinionated and do and follow what they believe is right. They crave to see raw and honest content and appreciate people who offer that.

Influencers, unlike celebrities, promote honesty and full disclosure, without sugarcoating reality for what it is. They promote a culture focusing on genuine and transparent opinions. They interact with their audience, which makes them all the more attractive to this generation. Companies have been struggling to grasp the attention of this demographic, investing vast sums of money in their marketing campaigns. They spend a lot on different types of advertisements in hopes to get this audience to respond. Influencers form the bridge between companies and their target audience as they often provide tangible results through their intangible efforts.

It is essential to denote that influencer marketing must benefit both the company and the influencer; it cannot be one-sided. When influencers are making all the efforts to promote a brand, they should be paid their dues, and given creative freedom. It ensures that their content is unbiased and genuine, not some scripted advertisement.

Gen Z members have figured out how to create their own culture, economy, and place in the world. The old school thinking of going to college and getting a good education, working your way up the ladder for forty years, buying a home and building up your 401K just so you can pay for your own kid's college and weddings, and then retire quietly in a small community in Florida playing pickleball is definitely not for the Zoomers. Creating a gig economy, not having six-figure student loan debt, learning to code, and create content to share is the Zoomer way. Build your social media platform following up large enough, and you've become an influencer. Gen Z'ers are consumers **AND** creators.

There is a rapid shift in the digital landscape, and any brand that has not been keeping up is only wasting its ad budgets, shrinking its market shares, and losing customers. As long as the influencers a brand is using have a good reputation and loyal audience, their precise number of followers becomes irrelevant. What matters is how favorably their audience reacts and responds to their recommendations. Take a closer look at true brand enthusiasts. After cultivating a rock-solid relationship with them, they should be given the room to mold the content in their own way.

Chapter 14: Sponsorship And Authentic Embedding Of Product Placement

I asked Jonathan Sumers, Senior Director of Esports Operations for the Cleveland Cavaliers what his favorite esports moment was. As the head of an NBA 2K team, he had to have plenty of memorable events he's been a part of. He shared that his favorite esports moment occurred the first time he went to an in-person esports competition. As he shares, "It was a sold-out Barclays Center in Brooklyn, New York with 20,000 fans standing and cheering the entire time. I was not expecting the level of excitement and engagement that I witnessed. I walked away from that event realizing that esports is here to stay and will only get bigger."

Brands gravitate to eyeballs and esports is delivering a huge audience and an extremely passionate and enthusiastic fan base.

Esports is getting bigger all the time and sponsorship is a major component of that revenue growth. By definition, sponsorship is a business relationship between the provider of funds, services, or resources of an individual, organization, rights holder, or event. It offers some rights and associations in return, which may be used as a commercial advantage.

Through sponsorship, a business is allowed to show that it is affiliated to an event, organization, or person that it has chosen to support. The enthusiasts or patrons of that event, organization, or the individual being sponsored should either be current or prospective customers of the business. The central concept of sponsorship is for brands to develop a stronger bond or relationship among themselves and the customers, keeping the person, event, or organization being sponsored as a mediator. There are quite a few **objectives** of sponsorships. Here are a few important ones.

Gaining Publicity

In the news, media sponsorship is used to create a publicity opportunity. Major worldwide sporting events, such as football, tennis, and major golf tournaments, offer global media coverage. Millions of people around the world watch these events, and thus sponsoring them provides brands with international exposure. Some games have a more upmarket profile, like golf. These publicity opportunities for sponsors can produce vital awareness shifts. Moreover, it also helps create entertainment opportunities for customers by sponsoring music, performing arts, and sporting events. Successful employees, customers, and trade partners can be rewarded by offering tickets at sponsored events, referred to as hospitality in the industry.

Fostering Favorable Brand and Company Associations

If a brand sponsors a mega-event like the Soccer World Cup or the Olympics, they are bound to get instant international recognition. Sponsoring such events comes with a tremendous amount of prestige, and it helps boost the company's credibility. As soon as a company associates with an event that huge, they advance to the big league. Everyone knows that such sponsorships require vast sums of money, showing the worth and credibility of the brand. Having said that, if a company wants to foster favorable brand associations, it can also do so through the sponsorship of special events like charities or arts. The patrons of that event will view the company favorably, and they may also put a positive word out about the company in their social gatherings.

Improving Community Relations

It is always a good idea to sponsor an event or organization that will ultimately help the community where the event is being organized or taking place. This form of sponsorship is usually called cause marketing. Sponsorship can be of anything, even with schools, by giving them low-cost computers and supporting their community programs. These efforts show that a brand is socially responsible. The most common objective of sponsorship is developing community relations for both consumer and industrial companies. There are usually various opportunities available for sponsorships in all communities.

Creating Promotional Expenditure

This incorporates things like bags, pens, hats, and other chachkies that carry the company's logo and the event's name, which can be sold to a captive audience. Banners and flags that have the company's name written on them can be displayed at the event site and even outside it. When companies sponsor events, this is particularly vital. Customers often have the opportunity to sample brand products where they can consume them during the event.

Sponsorship vs. Advertisement

People often wonder what is the difference between sponsorship and advertisement because they tend to seem quite similar, if not the same. However, they are actually vastly different. While a sponsorship means that a company is creating an ongoing relationship with a person or an event, advertisement is more or less transactional, and quite straight forward with a singular message. Advertisements focus on providing information about the product or service with the purpose of a compelling buying event. They do not focus primarily on getting personal with the audience. They are bent on making an impact or grasping the audience's attention, done through different mediums like television, radio, and social media. However, at the same time, people tend to get annoyed by them because they feel intrusive, especially to the younger generations of Millennials and Gen Z.

Sponsorships, on the other hand, are far from ads. They create a bond and an affinity between the brand and the target audience through an association with an organization or a property.

When it comes to sponsorship, the consumer creates an attachment to the brand that goes emotionally deep because the brand supports something the consumer cares about. Advertisements, on the other hand, are just a single one-directional message with no bonding with the consumer whatsoever. While they are both marketing tools, one is louder about the fact that it wants the consumer's money while the other is subtly telling them that they care by associating with an event that the attendees are passionate about. That is what people want to hear and feel today – that others around them care about the same causes or interests as them, support similar things, and so on.

Another way of marketing to this demographic is through product placement. Let's look into what that means and how brands use it to reach Gen Z better.

What is Product Placement?

In simple words, product placement means placing a certain brand in media content to influence the consumer's behavior. Companies typically pay a movie or television show producer a sum of money to have their brand or product displayed during the movie or show for some time. This, in turn, creates a positive brand image because it influences the customers' perception. An example of product placement in a TV program can be seen through American Idol. In the show where the panel of judges sits, they each have a red glass with the Coca-Cola logo on it placed in front of them. Everyone from the contestants to the audience is exposed to these glasses, which not only increases brand image but also makes people likelier to purchase that brand's products because of their affinity for the show.

Moreover, this can be quite effective when it comes to Gen Z, as they are a generation that binge-watches their favorite shows on Netflix and Amazon Prime. This has become the new advertising avenue for advertisers. When it comes to product placement, it is seen under the light of the relationship between the product and the brand. While the visible attributes are represented by the product, the brand reflects the guarantee of quality. The consumers are provided with the benefits of the brand's strength through the visual message. To the brand, there are different associations related to it, ranging from philosophy, vision, and characteristics of the typical buyer. It may include personality traits or age groups. In product and brand placement, the primary purpose of positioning a brand is to explain how a sustainable competitive advantage can be created by the brand in the minds of customers. The target remains to gain customer loyalty and ensure profits and increased revenue.

Is Product Placement Effective?

A study was conducted on 220 undergraduate respondents of the age bracket of 18-24 years. They were given questionnaires to determine the answer to this question. The fact of the matter is that as a marketing communication tool, one of the main concerns, when it came to product placement, was whether consumers were even aware of product placement. Marketers and advertisers deliberately place their products and services in visual content, and it costs money as well. Thus, the research intended to find out whether the realism of the film and respondents' recognition of branded products placed in a movie increased through product placement.[31]

The university-based respondents completed the questionnaire, and were exposed to film stimuli containing product placements. The findings stated that product placements in films positively affect the realism aspect of a movie. When branded products are placed in films, it injects a sense of realism into them. It's kind of like when TV shows always used to use a phone number like 555-5555 in their show. Everyone knows it's a fake number, and because it is, for that split moment, it breaks the realism of the show.

Moreover, another conclusion drawn was that brand recognition was prompted in movies through product placement. The findings and conclusions of this study emphasize that the prominence of product placement in film affects consumers' ability to see the product in question. The more prominent the movie and the placement are, the greater the chances that consumers will observe it. It is recommended that sales and marketing executives should carefully position their products in film and television programs to ensure the desired effect. Another study[32] conducted in June 2018 found that Gen Z supports product placement. The data of the study showed that Gen Z is the one with the strongest opinions about product placement. All this data and much more suggests that

---

[31]Van der Waldt, De la Rey & Ls, Du & Toit, R & Redelinghuys, (2007). Does branded product placement in film enhance realism and product recognition by consumers? African Journal of Business Management. 1. 19-25.

[32] *Go With What You Know: Gen Z Prefers Product Placements Over Traditional Advertising* Retrieved from
https://civicscience.com/go-with-what-you-know-gen-z-prefers-product-placements-over-traditional-advertising/

Generation Z actually does not mind product placement, and if anything, they resonate with it. They feel more connected to the brands when they see those products in a movie or show. This is how brands create an indirect but authentic relationship with them. Obviously, this has major significance when it comes to esports and product placement that can happen right within the gaming environment.

As an example, NFL partner Pizza Hut became the first brand to sign a virtual stadium naming rights deal with EA Sports for the Madden '21 championship series. Joining Pizza Hut as sponsors of MADDEN '21 were NFL official marketing partners SNICKERS, Oakley, Gillette, and Campbell's Chunky – creating an incredibly diverse non-endemic sponsorship roster. Sponsors' roles have been significantly expanded from mere signage or banner ads, with each being deeply integrated into the game itself through bespoke branded experiences.

The evidence of major brands getting involved in esports comes from the highest levels of gaming and sports. As Vida Mylson, Sr. Director of Commercial Brand Partnerships at EA SPORTS, shared at the Madden '21 release announcement, "Coming off the biggest product year in the history of the franchise and the star-studded, entertainment-driven evolution of MCS programming, *Madden NFL 21* has stepped onto an elevated platform of opportunity for brand partnerships in the world of competitive gaming. Alongside this world-class roster of sponsors, all connected by our affiliation to the NFL, we'll deliver new and authentic brand experiences that fuel football culture and resonate with the next generation of gaming fans."

Having discussed a few different types of advertising, there is another effective type we must explore. This is known as micro-targeting. It is a strategy of marketing in which detailed consumer data and demographics are used to create audience segments and subsets. It helps brands predict what the buying behavior of these like-minded individuals would be, ultimately influencing that behavior by doing hyper-targeted advertising.

How does micro-targeting work in advertising?

Let's assume that a brand's end goal is someone purchasing their service or product. The first thing they will have to do is identify the attributes and actions of people who already purchased the products. Secondly, they gather data about them, for instance, their location, age, income, education, etc. Lastly, additional more specific attributes like pet owners, travel enthusiasts, games, and others can be layered on for greater detail.

Go Deep into Your Big Data

When these specific characteristics are identified and overlapped, it creates unique subsets of a broader audience. It can be used to easily identify like-minded customers who share those specific traits. When a brand does that, they can build an entirely new audience of potential customers who have not only already purchased their product or service but also share similar consumer shopping trends. The key here is quality over quantity and how the data can be used by marketers to predict which consumers are likelier to make a purchase.

The Payoff of Micro-targeted Advertising

After dividing the audience like that, brands can easily focus a portion of their digital dollars on this specific audience, using relevant messaging to reach a niche market. Consumer-first marketing – as opposed to a spray and pray plan – describes what campaigns must communicate to tired buyers in a personal way. Micro guidance gives marketers big data, which can be used to create a broader audience profile. It allows firms to create personalized messages for different consumer groups. They can even be separated for different devices, ensuring maximum outreach and impact. It plays a massive role when it comes to campaign management efforts. If there is one big disruptive trend that has affected advertising the most in the last decade, it is the collection and availability of large amounts of consumer data.

Advantages of Micro Marketing
Highly Targeted

The best part about micro-marketing is that it is specific to detail. It targets unique market segments and can reach them at incredible speed using the most optimized devices and carriers for their messages. The demographics are being drilled down to a specific segment of the population, based on their sex, interests, ethnicity, location, and even things like their favorite foods.

Cost-Effective

While this marketing is not an inexpensive marketing method in its entirety, when compared to other approaches that target huge audiences, it can offer cost-effect solutions. Companies and brands can put their ad dollars ideally in specifically targeted ways when using this branding technique.

User-Generated Growth

All micro-marketing campaigns have to do is plant seeds in specific areas. The onus is then left to the early adopters to take a step. When people find something they love, they do not hesitate to tell others in their life about it. It often creates a snowball effect.

Disadvantages of Micro Marketing
High Cost Per Acquisition

While compared to other marketing strategies, this type does not take much of a brand's advertising budget. However, the number of people being targeted is fewer compared to a macro-marketing campaign. This may increase the average cost of getting a new customer.

Possibility of Missing the Target

Since micro-marketing campaigns are narrowly targeted, it might be harder for a company to make it right the first time. Micro-campaign tends to use a shotgun approach. It will hit many people but may miss all of them if they are not close.

Time-Consuming

These campaigns, since so rich in data, take time to develop. They require time and effort to plant roots in prospects. With effort, they can spread further than just the initial target. However, they are time-consuming and may not wield any profits overnight. Sure, the customer base formed in the end may be loyal, but it comes at a cost.

Advertising in Gaming

When it comes to Generation Z, the marketing opportunities are countless. More than anything, online gaming has been on the rise in this demographic. While there was once a time TV advertising was how brands could easily connect with young audiences, it is now on the decline. Only 33% of Gen Z watches TV, and a little over half of the Millennials have a satellite TV subscription or a cable. While a part of the reason for this may be the fact that they choose online streaming networks like Netflix, video games have been moving up in the advertising world.

Gaming is more than entertainment

When it comes to Gen Z, gaming is not just an escape or a source of entertainment. It is crucial in connecting the newest generation to their friends. Take the example of Fortnite. A huge reason for its popularity is due to the fact that it helped connect real-life friends with one another as they played in different locations. Many people simply downloaded the game because their friends were playing it too.

When we look at this under the advertisement lens, it tells us a lot about how creative marketing in the gaming industry works to reach and get through to Gen Z. The community appeal of Fortnite works quite well for users of this demographic as the virtual and real relationships are intertwined for them. Advertisers must take a step back and ask themselves whether the brand they have is perceived reachable and friendly by the Gen Z user base. Once they answer this, it will help them understand whether this generation will identify with the brand's products and ideologies. Moreover, they should also consider using gaming channels to emulate offline connections with their target audience.

The rise of gaming as a channel of advertisement

A reclusive teenage boy sitting in Mom's basement is no longer the face of a typical gamer. Over 70% of players are older than 18 years, and the male to female ratio is also almost even. Gamers are not specified to a particular ethnicity or race. They are diverse in many different ways. Generation Z is full of kids who grew up with gaming consoles and controllers in their hands. Gaming is literally a part of who they are. They use it to connect and communicate with like-minded friends and tend to influence one another, too.

Thanks to all the technological advancements, gaming has finally gone big. Devices are equipped with high connectivity and offer games that one can play anywhere at any time. The gaming industry is now ten times bigger than it was before, and esports and streaming keep gaining popularity by the day. With 90% of the US teens hooked to their consoles, gaming has now become a great medium for advertising and reaching Gen Z.

Take esports superstar Ninja as an example. In 2018, he held a Red Bull sponsored Fortnite event, which sold out literally within a matter of minutes. The next year, he had his own line of an extensive collection of limited-edition Red Bull cans. When he collaborated with Adidas, it took only an hour for his sneakers to be completely sold out. Ninja has become the LeBron James of esports, where sponsorship earnings are more than tournament winnings or esports earnings.

Marketers should use this example to understand how these gamers have a strong buying power with disposable income. As we've stated before, this mobile-first generation has over $143 billion in spending power. It helps gaming create one-of-a-kind opportunities for brands. Advertisers must improve their game and think about how they can communicate with a fast-paced generation. This generation is used to very image-heavy environments, and brands must use that to their advantage.

Viewability

Gaming provides an action-focused environment that directs the player's full attention as their eyes survey the screen, capturing every detail. This is where ad views can be integrated seamlessly into the gaming environment as 100% of observations and details are followed intently. Advertisers know when a player passes through a board or marker with a brand name as he has hit the corner in this racing game. Brands can get aggregate data on the appearance of the ad, how long the ad was viewed, and whether they are viewed forwards, sideways, or are slightly visible due to the inconvenience. This ability to measure ROI far surpasses the ability to measure traditional digital pop-up or banner ads.

Targeting

Console providers and video game publishers have the liberty to collect data on every player while they ensure that the highest standards of data privacy are maintained at the same time. With that being said, many players are willing to share their personal data just for the sake of a better and more personalized experience. It helps advertisers deliver campaigns that are hyper-targeted, served programmatically, and in real-time. When they have tiny details about the players, marketers can create effective and personalized campaigns. For example, Taco Bell's logo could be placed on a team's jersey around dinner time, which may subconsciously affect a player's meal choices. Kind of like how you always see food commercials on late-night television just as you are falling asleep and your brain is drifting off into subliminal Theta waves.

Authenticity

Everyone despises those pesky distracting ads! When an ad has a negative impact on the user, it loses its value. Due to the premium nature of the games and technologies that allow the ads to be placed on any item within the game itself, they can look natural and similar to how they would appear in real life. Forced or projected branding does NOT work with this generation.

For instance, an embedded advertisement within the game itself seems natural and not forced. Video games are essentially at their core simulations of real life, and advertisements strategically placed within those games where one would ordinarily and naturally see them in the real world makes this type of advertisement welcome and authentic. Companies that would not be able to run campaigns on an arena's jumbo screen at an NBA live game due to cost constraints can take advantage of the gaming opportunity to deliver their message to the most engaged players using the video game, NBA 2K.

The bottom line is that advertising comes in all shapes and sizes, and the trends keep changing by the day. If a brand or company really wants to stay connected to any specific generation or demographic, they must remain in the loop and keep in touch with social trends. What people liked and responded to years ago is no longer that effective or relevant, for that matter. It is high time marketers understand that. They must up their game and target individuals in the subtlest manner so that they do not feel intruded upon by the advertisers' campaigns.

Chapter 15: Conclusion

"Brands targeting Gen Z need to look beyond the confines of traditional segmentation, the ultimate priority always has to be on alignment that helps us cultivate relationships with youth culture - not just organize it." — ***Gregg L. Witt***

Generation Z, as you must know by now, is unique and special in its own way. It is a generation of wild, spirited, real, and highly opinionated individuals. There are so many things to consider when marketers target this demographic. They are people who have never seen a world that was safe, and they are not afraid to fight for what they believe in and support each other's beliefs. They have grown up a little too fast compared to the people of their age from previous generations.

This group started their young lives with a generational moment with the tragedy of 9/11, and then subsequently lived through mass school shootings one after another, a major recession, and the global pandemic. The world is a very scary place, and Gen Z has been asked to make their way in this unprecedented environment.

Generation Z is the most ethnically diverse generation in history. In the United States, nearly 50% of Gen Z are categorized as ethnic minorities. Social norms have flipped, and this generation is more likely to consider themselves inclusive and to challenge stereotypes. According to the Pew Research Center, this attitude is reflected in their purchasing habits as well. Well over 60% expect brands to align with and support causes that they agree with. Cause marketing resonates with this generation more than any other. Gen Z voters who are over 18 are more likely to describe themselves as independents as opposed to Republican or Democrat. Gen Z is also the most entrepreneurial generation yet. Over 40% of Gen Z want to work for themselves, and over 60% of college students want to start their own businesses. The influencer generation has exploded, and as Gen Z consumes massive amounts of media and content, they see influencers who have built a following and a healthy income out of social media platforms such as Instagram and Tik Tok, thereby disrupting the traditional corporate model of broadcasting one message to as many impressions or viewers and/or listeners as possible. In the "old days" of advertising, traditional influencers such as sports stars or celebrities were hired to promote brands.

These days, every single person who owns a smart phone is not only a consumer but also a potential creator, so traditional celebrity influencer marketing is being replaced with real people. According to Hubspot, social media posts that have a relevant image or video garner 94% more engagement than posts without. Visual content is king, and those images or quick videos appeal to Gen Z, who are accustomed to digesting information quickly and in large quantities of short bursts.

There are quite a lot of differences among all the different generations. Before targeting and approaching any generation, a company or brand must learn to understand everything about them – from their heartfelt stories to what makes them tick, and how they are different from the other generations. Coming back to Generation Z, we find that esports is one of the keys to reaching this group. It is a global phenomenon. The world Gen Z knows is much different from what the world was a few decades ago. The values they have instilled within themselves are much different from those of their parents or grandparents.

Years ago, marketing and advertising options were pretty limited, with various subsets of traditional marketing being the only way to reach out to consumers. Brands were limited to promoting their products through radio and television ads and billboards. While traditional advertising has not died down entirely yet, there are countless marketing opportunities available today. They range from traditional ways to digital marketing through social media advertisements, influencers, targeted advertisements, product placements, and most importantly, through esports.

The fact of the matter is that Generation Z craves authenticity and hates their privacy being disrupted. At the same time, they love personalization. In a time like this, when targeting a generation like theirs, advertisers must be cautious while marketing to them. A little inappropriate or offensive content can ruin a brand's entire credibility to this generation. Moreover, if they see an advertisement too many times, they don't get brainwashed, they simply get annoyed by that brand.

Marketing to Generation Z is like walking on a very fine tight rope, one wrong step, and you might crash into a brick wall with no chance at recovery. Advertisers, therefore, can create actual partnerships with popular esports influencers to reach out to this generation and create a relationship with them. Additionally, they can also sponsor esports events to create brand awareness on a larger scale and find ways to authentically embed their brand in the fabric of the experience.

At the end of the day, it all comes down to what the brand is selling, how large their marketing budget is, and who their target audience is. If a brand only wishes to target a specific niche, there is no need for them to do large scale marketing. They can simply opt for micro-advertising. Similarly, advertisers must understand and stay in touch with how the trends are changing. They should realize how the power of influence is no longer in the hands of famous celebrities but lies with regular people creating and interacting with their peers on mobile devices.

People no longer care about fake personas and air-brushed pictures. They want to see real, raw, and honest. They want to see all the good and bad, as they know that the world is not all rainbows and sunshine. They want to see vulnerability. They want to feel like they are looking in a mirror and seeing themselves. Gen Z is most accepting of this reality. They are strong mental health advocates who have seen more depression than the rest of the generations.

To gain popularity among this demographic, brands can also stand for similar causes like mental health, homophobia, and racism. They must remember that these people are not afraid of fighting for their rights, regardless of how loud they may have to be. Also, they will not let their voices be hushed. All brands have to do is be on the same wavelength as them and ride the same waves they do. They may sound complicated as a generation, but they are not. They just do not like inauthentic polished sales pitches.

With information being at their fingertips, they always do extensive research before choosing a brand. If a brand wants Gen Zers to stick with them, they must prove their loyalty to them. They want to see that brands care about them, and that is when they return the favor. They do not play one-sided games.

Generation Z spends hours gaming on their mobile phones or gaming consoles. Esports has really evolved over the years, quickly expanding from that very first tournament to become a global phenomenon, where millions of people stream virtual sporting events. Many brands are already making quite a lot of money through esports with increased revenues and sales. Esports is a market that will continue to gain in popularity exponentially.

Gen Z wants to hear stories, as they seek authenticity and emotional attachment. When targeting them, brands must ensure that whatever they are advertising, it should be impactful. It should stand in line with their beliefs because only then will they resonate with the brand. Having said all of that, the other generations still hold their own importance too. Whether they are the Baby Boomers or Millenials, each one of them is unique in their own way, and marketers should not forget about them either. It's just the fact that, currently, Gen Z is on a meteoric rise with substantial influence and buying power. By the year 2021, millions of Gen Zers will have entered the workplace and will hold $3 trillion dollars in purchasing power. The previous generations have had their time, but the thunder is now transferred onto Gen Z quicker than ever due to technology and the lightning speed pace of the world today. They are the future sooner than any generation that came before them.

I hope this book taught you all the concepts I have tried to squeeze into these pages. My desire is that you benefit greatly from it, and it helps you see advertising to the new generations in a whole new light. I have written it to-the-point, and no chapter is interlinked to one another. Therefore, you can either read the book in one go or simply take it chapter-wise and use it as an esports reference repository as it suits you.

With more knowledge about your market audience breakdown and a deep dive into the Gen Z demographic, hopefully, you can create better and more effective advertising and sponsorship campaigns. Targeting esports is an obvious bridge to the latest generation with significant buying power. The esports market is explosive and untapped. First movers will, as always, hold a significant advantage.

CODA

I had the pleasure of being the keynote speaker at one of the marquee esports conferences, the **Casino Esports Conference** held every year in Las Vegas. The conference was hosted at the amazing Hyper X esports arena, located in the Luxor hotel right on the strip. The Hyper X arena is an incredible 30,000 square-foot multi-level venue dedicated to esports competitions and gaming. With a full broadcast center, production studio, luxury VIP lounges, and a 50-foot LED video wall on the gaming stage, this arena is a testament to the growth and popularity of esports competitions. My keynote was on the topic of "Sponsorships and Esports," and I had an enjoyable time sharing a lot of the thoughts and insights that are included in this book. At the Q&A part of the session at the end, the Chief Marketing Officer (CMO) of a very well known Fortune 500 brand stood up at the microphone and asked simply, "Why esports?"

A million bullet points and statistics immediately popped into my head on how to answer. (The thought of "weren't you just listening for the past sixty minutes" also briefly crossed my mind, but fortunately, the little man with the stop sign in my head blocked me from blurting that out.)

Reflecting back on thinking of how to answer the question **Why Esports**, I could have pointed out that at the end of 2020, according to data analytics company Statista, the global esports market was valued at $950 million dollars with a projected global esports market revenue reaching $1.6 billion US dollars by 2023. To answer the question **Why Esports,** I could have also pointed to an analysis by Newzoo that predicts the annual growth rate of esports viewing will be approximately 10.4%. They expect that the number of casual viewers will grow to 351 million and that there will be another 295 million esports hardcore enthusiasts, making the total audience 646 million. For brands that covet eyeballs, that's a mind popping number. A great answer to **Why Esports** could easily be that the reasons for the optimism in this expected growth in esports viewership is simply because more people are learning about it. In the past five years, there has been a tremendous rise in the awareness of esports. Additionally, the rise of platforms and outlets offering live esports coverage is also increasing. YouTube Gaming had its best year ever according to 2020 statistics with more than 100 billion hours watched, doubling its viewership in just two years. Another obvious answer to the CMO's question of **Why Esports** is that brands have pivoted to covet content creation, and it's a fact that creators across the board have seen massive increases in subscribers, audiences, and viewership in just the last year. And part of the reason why that gaming content has likely exploded in 2020 is the ongoing coronavirus pandemic! Online activity stats for activities like streaming television and multiplayer gaming have gone through the roof. Because everyone was stuck at home during the global pandemic, U.S. consumers spent more than $33 billion dollars on video games in the first three quarters of 2020 alone. All of those would have been pretty awesome and legitimate answers to the question **Why Esports.**

But when asked point-blank, **"Why Esports?"** the only answer that made the most sense to me was ....

Why not?

Bibliography

eSports market revenue worldwide from 2012 to 2022 Retrieved from
https://www.statista.com/statistics/490522/global-esports-market-revenue/

Millennials vs. Gen Z: How Are They Different? Retrieved from
https://www.salesforce.com/blog/2017/10/how-Millennials-and-gen-z-are-different.html

The Global Growth of Esports Retrieved from
https://cdn2.hubspot.net/hubfs/700740/Reports/Newzoo_Preview_R
eport_Global_Growth_of_Esports_Report_FINAL_2.0.pdf

Esports Viewership Retrieved from
https://www.roundhillinvestments.com/research/esports/esports-viewership-vs-sports

Twitch Revenue and Usage Statistics Retrieved from
https://www.businessofapps.com/data/twitch-statistics/#1

Esports becoming as popular as regular sports with younger Retrieved from
*generations*https://www.dailyesports.gg/esports-becoming-as-popular-as-regular-sports-with-younger-generations/

Female viewership of esports Retrieved from
increasinghttps://www.gamesindustry.biz/articles/2019-02-21-female-viewership-of-esports-increasing

Battle Royale: Everything you need to know Retrieved from
https://www.tomsguide.com/us/fortnite-battle-royale-faq,news-25928.html

How to play Fortnite Retrieved from https://www.gamesradar.com/how-to-play-fortnite/

What is League of Legends? Retrieved from
https://www.riftherald.com/2016/9/29/13027318/lol-guide-how-to-watch-play-intro

How Millennials compare to prior generations Retrieved from
https://www.pewsocialtrends.org/essay/millennial-life-how-young-adulthood-today-compares-with-prior-generations/

Pew Research Center, "Millennials in adulthood: Detached from institutions, networked with friends," March 7, 2014, Retrieved from
http://www.pewsocialtrends.org/2014/03/07/Millennials-in-adulthood/.

Deloitte, "Mind the gaps: The 2015 Deloitte Millennial Survey," 2015, Retrieved from http://www2.deloitte.com/global/en/pages/about-deloitte/articles/Millennialsurvey.html.

Department of Education, National Center for Education Statistics, Digest of Education Statistics, 2014, table 326.10, Retrieved from
https://nces.ed.gov/programs/digest/d14/tables/dt14_326.10.asp.

Department of Education, National Center for Education Statistics, Digest of Education Statistics, 2014, table 322.10, Retrieved from
https://nces.ed.gov/programs/digest/d14/tables/dt14_322.10.asp.

Department of Education, National Center for Education Statistics, Digest of Education Statistics, 1997, table 315, Retrieved from
http://nces.ed.gov/programs/digest/d97/d97t315.asp

Department of Education, National Center for Education Statistics, Digest of Education Statistics, 2014, table 331.20, Retrieved from
http://nces.ed.gov/programs/digest/d14/tables/dt14_331.20.asp.

William Frey, "Millennial and senior migrants follow different post-recession paths," Brookings Institution, 2013, Retrieved from
http://www.brookings.edu/research/opinions/2013/11/15-millennial-senior-post-recession-frey.

Megan Benetsky, Charlynn Burd, and Malanie Rapino, "Young adult migration: 2007–2009 to 2010–2012," US Census Bureau Report Number ACS-31, March 18, 2015, Retrieved from
http://www.census.gov/library/publications/2015/acs/acs-31.html.

How much Should Gen X and Millennials have saved? Retrieved from
https://www.forbes.com/sites/davidrae/2018/04/30/gen-x-Millennials-should-have-saved/#3e1131f02bd3

How Retailers Will Have to Adapt to Millennials' Spending Habits in 2018 Retrieved from https://www.gobankingrates.com/saving-money/savings-advice/Millennials-spending-habits-retailers/#4

Millennials, how they shop, and why they buy Retrieved from https://www.herosmyth.com/article/millennial-consumer-how-they-shop-why-they-buy

Ten new findings about the millennial consumer Retrieved from https://www.forbes.com/sites/danschawbel/2015/01/20/10-new-findings-about-the-millennial-consumer/#6233e4bf6c8f

Deep Focus' Cassandra Report: Gen Z Uncovers Massive Attitude Shifts Toward Money, Work and Communication Preferences Retrieved from https://www.globenewswire.com/news-release/2015/03/30/1308741/0/en/Deep-Focus-Cassandra-Report-Gen-Z-Uncovers-Massive-Attitude-Shifts-Toward-Money-Work-and-Communication-Preferences.html

The Value of CX: Why We Need To Start Talking About NPS Again Retrieved from https://www.visioncritical.com/gen-z-versus-millennials-infographics/

AI-READY OR NOT: ARTIFICIAL INTELLIGENCE HERE WE COME! Retrieved from http://www.webershandwick.com/uploads/news/files/AI-Ready-or-Not-report-Oct12-FINAL.pdf

Cutting through advertising clutter Retrieved from https://www.cbsnews.com/news/cutting-through-advertising-clutter/

Gen Z relies on influencers for purchase decisions, Kantar says Retrieved from https://www.mobilemarketer.com/news/gen-z-relies-on-influencers-for-purchase-decisions-kantar-says/573264/

Why young Americans follow influencers Retrieved from https://morningconsult.com/wp-content/uploads/2019/11/The-Influencer-Report-Engaging-Gen-Z-and-Millennials.pdf

The influence of influencers: new research unveiled Retrieved from https://www.gen.video/blog/the-influence-of-influencers-new-research-unveiled

Van der Waldt, De la Rey & Ls, Du & Toit, R & Redelinghuys, (2007). Does branded product placement in film enhance realism and product recognition by consumers? African Journal of Business Management. 1. 19-25.

Go With What You Know: Gen Z Prefers Product Placements Over Retrieved from *Traditional Advertising* https://civicscience.com/go-with-what-you-know-gen-z-prefers-product-placements-over-traditional-advertising/

Made in the USA
Middletown, DE
02 March 2022

62019637R00116